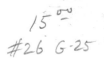

CREATURES OF THE SEA

Creatures of the Sea

by

CAPTAIN

William B. Gray

DIRECTOR OF COLLECTIONS AND EXHIBITIONS
MIAMI SEAQUARIUM

FREDERICK MULLER LIMITED

LONDON

FIRST PUBLISHED IN GREAT BRITAIN IN 1962 BY
FREDERICK MULLER LIMITED
PRINTED IN GREAT BRITAIN BY EBENEZER BAYLIS AND SON, LTD.
THE TRINITY PRESS, WORCESTER, AND LONDON

TO SALLY

ACKNOWLEDGEMENTS

I am especially indebted to George Vanderbilt, whom I have accompanied on many expeditions in the Atlantic and Pacific Oceans in pursuit of museum specimens and in scientific studies of marine life. These cruises led us over many new horizons into virgin fishing waters, where much of the material for this book was gathered.

I am also grateful to Leon Mandel, whom I accompanied on several extensive collecting trips under the auspices of the Field Museum of Chicago; to Mr. and Mrs. Michael Lerner for their consultations and contributions of photographs, and to Marine Studios and the Miami Seaquarium, as it was through these institutions that a great part of my collecting career was made possible.

Also I would like to thank Ruth Mitchell Van Zuyle and Rosser Huff, who assisted me in compiling these pages, as well as my many fishing friends who have contributed information and photographs.

To all these I acknowledge my most sincere appreciation.

WILLIAM B. GRAY

CONTENTS

ILLUSTRATIONS

I

Sharks Alive

WHEN you go out fishing for sharks, anything may happen. You may come back with all your fingers and toes—or you may not. But if you are an ordinary fisherman, all your troubles are over when you have killed the shark and can bring him back to show your friends. When, however, your job is to bring the shark back alive and with all the teeth in top slashing condition, the expedition has its element of danger right up to the moment when you part company with the shark.

As Director of Collections and Exhibitions at the Miami Seaquarium, I have to go out and bring sharks back alive several times a year. I have been doing this throughout a lifetime of collecting marine specimens, and the only sure thing about it is that no two trips are alike.

One morning shortly after the Seaquarium opened in 1955, I set out with my two assistants to bring in some more sharks. It promised to be a routine trip—as routine as they ever get—when we loaded our gear and smelled the morning air. Our boats lay by the dock at the Seaquarium. This is situated on Virginia Key, looking out over Biscayne Bay, on the southeast coast of Florida. We stood on the dock and looked out over the blue water—which seemed a little choppy that morning—towards Miami on the extreme right, Key Biscayne on the left, and the Bay ahead. The brilliance of the Florida sun made the shores and trees distinct and even shining. The brightness of the reflections from the water makes it necessary for me to wear tinted glasses continually, since most of the time I am looking at the sea.

The boat we were going to use was one I had specially designed for this work of collecting fish alive. The *Sea Horse* was a cabin cruiser with a very blunt square end and a hoist for raising and lowering equipment. Lashed alongside her was the *Sea Cow*, a live-well barge, which was almost completely hollow inside and filled with sea water in which to transport our sharks. In one side of her was a gate, which could be raised or lowered to allow for slipping the sharks into the live-well through the side, instead of hauling them over the gunwale.

In addition to the *Sea Cow* we had two skiffs, the *Sea Calf* and the *Sea Colt*. These, operated by outboard motors, would be used for attending to lines at a distance from the main boats, if that should be necessary.

Now you don't just decide one morning you'll go shark hunting and jump in your boat and go. It takes at least one day to get ready, and then when you are through, it takes another day to get unready. The chief preparation for this hunt was the laying of the set-line the previous day. This is a rope three-quarters of an inch in diameter and about half a mile long, on which there are at regular intervals twenty-five rings. A chain ending in a two-inch hook snaps into each ring. The hooks are baited before being sent down to tempt the sharks.

We coiled the line in the boat on the previous evening and took it out about four miles from the basin to the edge of the Gulf Stream, which flows very close to this part of Florida. We dropped an anchor at each end of the line and attached flag buoys so that we would know where to find the anchors the next day. Then we left, hoping that the sharks would be in a hungry mood.

There are about three hundred and fifty kinds of sharks in the world, nearly fifty of which may be found off the coast of Florida. Only a few of these types are commonly met with, however, and fewer still will live very long in captivity.

On our twenty-five hooks we could expect to find about six or eight sharks. Of these one or two would die on the way to the Seaquarium or shortly after arrival and at the end of a month maybe two would still be alive. Because of this high mortality rate, we have to go out hunting about every six weeks, if we wish to keep the Seaquarium stocked with the usual fifty to one hundred sharks.

In spite of their reputation for ferocity, sharks are extremely delicate creatures to handle. They are not true fish, but belong to the same family as rays and sawfish, whose skeletons consist of cartilage rather than bones. For this reason handling sharks disturbs their inner organs very quickly. Their low intelligence, furthermore, makes them liable to panic, and it is this that makes them dangerous. In panic they use their five rows of sharp-edged teeth. Since just one of these teeth can shave the hairs off a man's arm, it is well to keep out of their reach.

The smell of blood attracts sharks into an area which otherwise they would probably not visit. It doesn't much matter what is bleeding; a shark will attack it at once, even if it is another shark. This attraction to blood probably accounts for the many tales of sharks attacking people who are in some way wounded.

With this knowledge, but also with years of experience in dealing with sharks, the three of us set out. The sea was definitely bumpy, and the going rather hard, but after about an hour we found the flag buoy we had set up the previous evening. Then we took up our positions as experience had taught us was best. The *Sea Horse* has two sets of controls, one on top of the cabin and another inside. I took the topside controls, since from this open position it would be easier to see what was happening to the line and to steer accordingly. My assistants, Emil Hanson and Edward Woodford, stood at the back of the boat and began pulling in the line, which they neatly coiled on the deck.

Four hooks came in empty—not only of sharks, but of bait. Some very cunning sharks had obviously learned how to get a good meal without getting caught. The fifth hook, however, was not empty. As both men heaved at the line, Woodford was nearly pulled overboard. Depending on their age and kind, sharks weigh anywhere from two pounds to over $6\frac{1}{2}$ hundredweight; this shark, which was nearly $6\frac{1}{4}$ hundredweight, was an unfair match for two men whose combined weight was only about 3 hundredweight,

As the men pulled their catch to the surface, we saw that it was a tiger shark—a type of shark which, like the lemon shark, ground shark, bull shark and nurse shark, is most commonly caught around Florida. Our fifteen-foot tiger shark was in such good condition that he would make a prize specimen, especially as a shark of his species stands a reasonable chance of survival in the Seaquarium.

But he did not like us at all. As soon as he was pulled up a little out of the water, he went into a panic and began thrashing about, diving, leaping and plunging. Suddenly he lurched downwards and pulled the line right underneath the boats. There was a great bumping and banging on the bottoms of the boats, and the motor sounded as though it was damaged. From my position on the top deck I saw all that happened. I quickly shut off the motor. I knew at once what the shark had done with the line: he had wound it round and round the propeller shaft as he thrashed about trying to get free.

Once the motor was off, only the struggles of the shark and the splashing of the boats in the choppy sea could be heard. At such a moment the comparative silence seems to magnify the menace beneath the surface. It is then that I pause for an instant and realize the great dangers of shark hunting.

But I could not pause for long, because other sharks were tugging at the main line and the one beneath the boat was demanding attention. The three of us tried to get the line off the propeller with the boathook, but it was too securely tied on. Emil Hanson looked over the side through a glass-bottomed bucket and reported that the shark had indeed put three turns of the line round the shaft and that he was swimming away in circles—all the time keeping the line stretched and taut.

In such circumstances it is necessary for someone to go under the boat and take the rope off the propeller by hand, while the others above keep watch for the shark. Emil Hanson put on his skin-diving equipment of face mask and snorkel (underwater breathing apparatus); we tied a line round his waist so that he could quickly be pulled to the boat if the situation turned nasty. I had a harpoon ready in case the shark should attack.

Woodford leaned over the side of the boat nearest the shark and watched as it circled. It was furious. There was a trickle of blood from its mouth where the hook had pierced the flesh. Its little eyes were on the watch for the enemy which had tied it to the line.

When it was circling farthest away from the boat, Woodford gave the signal to Hanson to go down and free the propeller. I held the safety line round his waist as well as the harpoon.

Although it seemed centuries in that silence, it was only a matter of minutes before Hanson broke the surface and gasped, "I've got one turn off."

Again we waited for the shark to move away on its line, which was now longer by a turn round the propeller shaft. Then Hanson went down again.

This time he was down longer, and the sweat stood out on our faces as we watched the manœuvring of the shark. But we knew Hanson had been successful when we saw it rush away with the free line. Hanson came up, and we pulled the line over the gunwale as fast as we knew how.

But there was no time for congratulation or relaxation. The shark had rushed downwards into the depth of the sea, and because the motor was still off, there was no force to help us pull against him. But all three of us, slowly pulling at the line, managed to bring the shark round to the side of the *Sea Cow*. When the shark was opposite the gate, we pulled it through into the live-well and unhooked the chain from the main line. As our flopping and fighting shark came into the live-well, Woodford leaned over and closed the gate.

There he was—fifteen feet of angry shark. Little did he know, as he tried to ruin our boat and our line, that he was being brought in to be treated with every kindness; he would be given any number of meals a day without having to fight for them.

We went back to our positions and all felt safer when the motor was started again. Woodford and Hanson went on hauling in the line, and the next catch was an eight-foot lemon shark—a comparative lightweight—who was soon steered into the barge to lie beside the tiger.

The next catch, however, was no lightweight; it was an enormous hammerhead shark, which must have weighed very nearly half a ton. Unfortunately he was dead, and a cannibal shark had eaten about a hundredweight of flesh just above his dorsal fin. The raw flesh, jagged and bleeding, was a sight to make us shudder and count ourselves very lucky in the scrape we had just been through.

Hammerheads get their name because their heads are formed like the metal part of a hammer, and their bodies correspond to the shaft. Their mouths are on the underside of the "hammer", and their eyes are at each end, so that they must see a completely different world with each eye. If we had captured our shark alive, he probably would not have lived very long, since the hammerhead species does not thrive in captivity. But dead or alive our gigantic specimen was rare enough to be worth having, so we heaved and strained and pulled its remains to the side of the boat. Since hauling him aboard would have been too much for us, we tied him up securely and towed him to the Seaquarium. The carcass was hung there for visitors to photograph.

After adding a ten-foot bull shark to the two in the live-well and then capturing some nurse sharks, which in captivity are the hardiest of the local species, we thought our day was nearly over. Our arms ached from pulling and straining, and the heavy sea had not made the boats any easier to control. But there was one more line to pull up.

From the topside controls I saw Hanson and Woodford in difficulty as they hauled it in: it was obvious that whatever shark we had there was a big one. I saw there was something unusual about the line, for it was being dragged around the boats. In order to pull the line like that, the shark must have been strong enough to lift the anchor at its end; and this is just what he had done. He was swimming round the boats, the anchor dragged behind him, and Woodford and Hanson had all they could do to hold on to the line.

Fearing another propeller incident, I stopped the motor and rushed down to help them. There wasn't much room: the half mile of main line (which we had hauled in as we worked) was coiled in the bottom of the boat, and all the hooks were there too, still attached. Just as I seized the rope to help hold the shark, it decided to plunge downwards. The lurch caught us all off our balance, and we sprawled on the gear. The shark, feeling the sudden lack of tension on the line as we all let go, took off as fast as he could, and the line began paying out after him. Before I could get up, one of the hooks caught in the belt of my shorts, and they were pulled right off. Although I was indignant at being undressed by a shark, I was glad that the shorts, rather than I, had gone over the side.

As we all regained our balance, we managed to grip the rope and stop the shark's rush. Since with or without shorts I had to take part in the fight, my appearance was ignored. Before, we had been frightened that the shark had pulled up the anchor, but now we were glad, for the weight slowed him down, and in twenty minutes of holding hard to the rope we were able to bring him alongside. Until now we had not been able to get a look at what we had, but as it came, still fighting, to the edge of the *Sea Cow*, we saw a tiger shark about as big as our first one. Our efforts had been well rewarded.

We had been tired before this last hook; we were now exhausted. Gratefully we pulled up the anchor and headed home, as our cargo of live sharks flopped and turned in the live-well of the barge beside us.

The sea was still quite bumpy, so we waited until we got into calmer water before we began to remove the hooks, which, with the chains attached to them, were still in the sharks' mouths.

Sharks are the only fish from which we make a practice of removing the hook. We leave the hook in smaller fish, partly because to remove it would cause more injury to the fish than would be wise, and partly because the hook soon removes itself by dissolving. The chemical salts of sea water and the liquids of the fish's own body will react upon the metal of the hook so quickly that in a few days it will crumple like paper and drop away. But a shark is caught with a huge two-inch hook, which requires a great deal of dissolving. Even if we remove the hook, we cannot avoid a large wound in the fish's mouth. We like to get the hook in the side of the mouth, where least harm is done; if it is lodged in the back of the throat, we do not even bother to bring the shark in, for it will die from loss of blood.

Having found it best not to try to get anything out of a shark's mouth by hand, I have, over the years, developed two devices for removing these hooks more safely. One of these "unhookers" is intended to push the hook back through the shark's mouth, and the other is supposed to pull it through forward. The first is a three-foot iron pole with a groove in a curve at the end. The curve corresponds precisely to that of the fish hook. You stand above the shark in the live-well, put the groove against the hook where it is protruding from the shark's jaw, and push. The hook then goes back through the mouth the way it came, and you can pull it up by means of the chain attached to it. The other device is used when the hook is embedded very deeply, or in a position not readily accessible to the grooved device. This second device consists of a small half-circle on the end of a rod. To use it you have to get closer to the shark than you would with the grooved curve because you must first cut the link of the chain nearest to the shark's mouth. (The cutting is easily done with wire snippers.) Then you push the half-circle against the barbs of the hook and pull the hook right through the jaw, along with any links of chain still attached.

Using the two implements, Hanson and I removed the hooks as gently as possible, for we did not want to lose any of the sharks which had cost us so much labour to catch. While Woodford was at the controls, we soon got the hooks out, even though the boat was rocking a little. We headed back to the Seaquarium to transfer our sharks as quickly as possible to a tank where they would have room to swim. Even though we go out shark hunting for five or six days at a stretch, we return each evening to bring in the captives, for they cannot live long in confined quarters.

When we arrived at the dock, the Seaquarium's maintenance crew came out to help. They hoisted a huge coffin-like box from the triangular hoist on the dock and swung it over the live-well in the *Sea Cow*. Standing by the live-well, we caught the box, lowered it inside and tipped it on its side. I jumped into the well and pushed one shark into the box. It was twisting and turning all the time, and the others kept rubbing against my legs. (The skin of a shark is rough like sandpaper, and can scratch quite painfully if it rubs very hard against you.) Fortunately I was soon able to persuade the twisting shark back into its box, and it was hauled up and placed on the back of a truck. We all went with it to see it placed in its tank, for we now had another task to perform before we could leave our sharks. We had to walk them.

The walk takes place in a specially shallow tank used for the orientation of fish which have just been caught. We seize the shark by its fins and walk round and round the tank with it to force water through its gills. For when a shark has been fought, captured, tossed around in the live-well, and manhandled into and out of a box, it often loses interest in life. When put in the tank, it will just roll over, show its white underbelly and its grinning mouth, and prepare to die. Then we step in, turn it right side up, and walk round with it, until it feels the water flowing through its gills and the blood pumping in its body. After about half an hour, it will carry on and swim on its own—if we're lucky. Sometimes we aren't and then we have to haul out a dead body.

But the greatest single problem in keeping fish in captivity is getting them to eat; the strangeness of the surroundings apparently leads them to suspect any food that is offered. Some fish overcome this suspicion, while others never do. Sharks, who are the camels of the ocean, can store enough vitamins in their livers to exist for as much as two or three months in the ocean without food. In captivity they have no need to eat for about a month, but some of them go without food for such a long time that they eventually die of starvation. Once a shark does take food, however—usually within a week after his capture—we put him in the main tank, where he joins other fish in the most natural setting possible in an aquarium. There he rarely gives us trouble, because he is content and well fed.

It does happen, however, that sharks die of what I think is claustrophobia: although the tank is quite large enough for their needs, they cannot tolerate the walls. In captivity they seem to have difficulty judging distances and will often rush headlong into these walls. One of the few hammerheads we have brought in would hit the side of his hammer against some wire netting every time he swam round his circular tank. He never learned to steer clear of that netting and eventually he hurt himself so much on it that he died.

We have also had our troubles with sharks who showed dangerous flashes of temperament. On one occasion we were moving a number of them from one tank to another. Two of us were in the water, which had been lowered to about waist-deep so that we could manœuvre more easily. Around us were about a dozen sharks of various kinds, who, unhappy at being disturbed, were swirling about in panic. Without incident my assistant and I managed to push each of about eleven sharks into a box, in which they were safely hauled away. Then we came to a large bull shark. We threw a heavy nylon net over it and thought we'd got it. But we had reckoned without those five rows of razor-like teeth. All tangled up as it was in the meshes of the net, it managed to rip its way through and then it rushed at us. First it caught my assistant above the knee, where it left a nasty bite. As the blood flowed into the water the shark became maddened with the smell and charged at me. It slashed sideways at my right leg. I felt the stinging pain of a cut and had the impression of actually hearing the flesh tear. Both of us leaped for the ladder. It was of no use trying to get the bull shark out, for he was on the rampage. This time he had won. Both my assistant and I had to be stitched up, and my leg, which had fifty-five stitches, looked like a neat piece of sewing. Luckily we were out of action for only three weeks, and the shark left us nothing worse than a scar.

2

More Big Ones

SHARKS are by no means the largest or most spectacular fish to be found in a sea-water aquarium like the Miami Sea-quarium. We have porpoises, manta rays, jewfish, sea cows and many others, none of which may seem as dangerous as sharks, but all of which present difficulties in catching.

The jewfish—and no one knows why it is called by this name—is the largest member of the grouper family; it weighs anything from $2\frac{1}{2}$ to $6\frac{1}{2}$ hundredweight. Its bulk is a mottled grey with faint dark stripes, and its fins are black. Because of the spots on its head, it is sometimes called the spotted jew-fish. An enormous turned-down mouth, which gives it a very disapproving expression, will open wide enough to swallow a three-foot fish at one gulp. And the jewfish, sitting at the bottom of his reef, is not too particular what sort of fish that is.

Because jewfish are sedentary by nature, they make an easy target for spear fishermen, who indeed don't show much skill in spearing them. I am frequently disgusted at the senseless destruction these fishermen call sport. On one occasion I found a huge jewfish sitting at the bottom of a reef off the southern Florida coast. Not having enough equipment to deal with him, since he weighed at least $4\frac{1}{2}$ hundredweight, I decided to leave him until the next day. I knew well that he would probably not move. Next day when I returned he hadn't moved; he couldn't—there were more than eight spears in him.

In 1955, when we were looking for at least six jewfish to stock the Seaquarium, the spear fishermen must have been at work. We looked in all the holes and caves at the bottom of reefs within a fifty-mile radius of Miami, but the jewfish were not in their old haunts. I began to wonder what to do, for we did not want the Seaquarium to be without these fish.

We were forced to go farther afield than we usually do for specimens. I got a tip from an old friend of mine, who used to catch jewfish commercially—for they make good eating—off Key West. When I flew there to talk to him, my friend showed me on a chart a deep reef in eighteen to twenty fathoms of water about eighteen miles off the Key. There he was sure we would find our jewfish.

So I returned to Miami and made ready the *Sea* fleet—the *Horse*, the *Cow*, the *Colt*, and the *Calf*. In three days we were at the spot my friend had suggested and we soon located the reef by means of soundings. We sent down hand-lines—for there was no need to use the sports fisherman's apparatus of rod and reel—and used hooks baited with live bar-jacks, because the jewfish likes his bait alive. My friend, and Hanson and Woodford, my assistants, who would pull in the line if we got a bite, wore gloves to prevent the line from burning their hands.

When, shortly after we had sent down the lines, we did get a bite, the men grasped the line and prepared to raise a fish equal to twice their weight. It was a long way down to the bottom of the reef, and the jewfish did not want to rise. But slowly our pulling had its effect; we began to gain line. Then suddenly the tension gave way, and up popped the jewfish like a huge grey inflated balloon.

It was the wrong side up. If we had not known from experience what was the trouble, we might have thought our labour was in vain. But we knew that a fish which lives at great depths, as the jewfish does, stores oxygen in its air bladder and in its blood vessels. Naturally at such depths the pressure is very great, and the air is compressed. But when the fish is forced from its natural depth to the upper water, where the pressure is less, the air expands, and so the fish inflates.

There is, luckily, a very quick and easy way to deal with this problem. Just as we had done with the sharks, we led the upside-down fish into the live-well of the *Sea Cow*, and Woodford jumped into the well with a sharp knife in his hand.

Holding the fish steady with one hand, he inserted the knife through the flesh about five inches behind the pectoral fin into the air bladder. The compressed air hissed out just as if you had punctured a balloon.

You could almost see the relief on the fish's unhappy face. In a few minutes he was swimming in the live-well right side up, and the incision in his side caused him no pain or distress. Once an incision has been made, in fact, the fish can either live comfortably in shallow water or dive to his normal depths.

We caught and deflated another jewfish the same day, but no more were biting after that.

On the day after we had much better luck. The first jewfish I caught, a $4\frac{1}{2}$-hundredweight monster, had suffered so much from air compression that when we pulled him into the live-well, his stomach was protruding from his mouth. After his deflation, however, we pushed the maw back in place with the smooth handle of a net, and the fish suffered no after-effects.

Although it was very pleasant fishing with a hand-line and enjoying the sun on the waves, the results came rather too slowly for us at that time. So we tried another method. I have found throughout a career of collecting specimens for aquaria, museums, and scientists, that I must often improvise a new method to obtain my fish. Our tactics this time called for a co-operative effort. Woodford and Hanson put on their skin-diving equipment and looked for jewfish under the reef. I ran the outboard motor in the *Sea Colt* and hovered near them. When they found a suitable fish, they would surface and signal to me and then dive again to offer the fish bait attached to a line dangling from my boat.

As often as not the jewfish was only too glad to take food offered to him without his having to move, and as soon as the hook was firmly in his jaw, Woodford and Hanson would give me the signal to set the hook and pull away. I then used the pulling power of the *Sea Colt* to tow the fish after me. The light skiff, which bobbed about like a cork, often seemed a rather unequal match for the weight of the fish. Although the motor churned furiously, the boat would sometimes go forward, sometimes sideways, and sometimes backwards. We all enjoyed the performance immensely and were very gratified when we found the method worked. Jewfish after jewfish popped to the surface, was deflated, and joined his fellows in the live-well. In one day we captured ten large ones.

Since six of our total of twelve did not recover completely from their experiences, we took them to the dock at Key West, where my friend who had acted as our guide could sell them. The others we took back to the Seaquarium, where, since they are not very highly-strung fish, they were not long in beginning to eat. Two of them did not live long, but three of them are still to be seen clinging closely to the rocks in the main tank of the Seaquarium.

What about the last? He was the object of a great deal of public interest in 1958 when an underwater operation was performed on him in the Seaquarium's main tank. A doctor and a nurse put on diving masks and went down to remove what looked like a growth on his belly. They worked at an underwater operating table, surrounded by divers armed with spears to keep away inquisitive sharks. After the jewfish had been tranquillized and given a local anaesthetic, the doctor made an incision in his side, extracted the object which had caused the bump and stitched up the wound. The fish was released from the table and put in a separate tank to recover.

It was not a growth which had necessitated the operation, but a weight from a diver's belt. When they enter a tank of water, divers wear belts of lead weights so that they will sink to the bottom and stay there. Obviously one of these lead weights had slipped out of a belt, and the jewfish had idly swallowed it after picking it up off the floor of the tank. In time it had worked its way through his stomach wall and lodged in the flesh. It is probable that if left alone, it would have eventually worked through the flesh and outside skin and dropped out, and the wound might then have healed as the stomach wall had clearly done.

After the operation the fish suffered no ill effects from the incision, but it died in about eight hours as a result of the anaesthetic. Very little is known about the effects of anaesthetic or tranquillizers on cold-blooded creatures, so the death of the unlucky jewfish did contribute a little to science.

Another fish which has challenged our attempts to collect it is the giant manta ray—also called devilfish. The manta ray, which is related to the shark and sawfish but has no true bones in its body, is an enormous flat creature, which looks like a great bat as it waves its huge wings to swim. Its tail is incongruously thin—rather like the tail of a kite—but it steers the huge body very accurately. The ray has a very large mouth with flapping "arms" jutting out on each side; these arms are, in fact, cephalic fins, which can be curled or opened out at will. By waving the arms in front of his mouth, the ray can attract into it enormous quantities of the plankton and small crustacea which he feeds upon.

Since the ray is usually too large to be easily captured and transported to an aquarium, I was very delighted one day to find a reasonably small one—about ten or twelve feet across—cruising below the surface not far from the Seaquarium. I have now forgotten exactly what we had taken the *Sea Horse* out for that day. But a collector must seize every chance that comes along; if he happens to be out for jellyfish, he can't disregard a whale!

The manta we discovered was about ten feet deep, near the edge of the Gulf Stream. As my assistant slowed down the boat, I stood ready in the prow with a harpoon. I wanted to strike the ray in the wing to avoid harming any vital section of its body, but to give us a firm enough hold to bring it in. Luckily the harpoon flew well and the dart went through the right wing about two feet from the tip. The toggle on the harpoon pulled tight, and at once the manta took off, as fast as he could swim.

Before I knew what had happened, I had no harpoon line left. All 600 feet of it were stretched behind the ray, who was pulling so hard that I was forced to let go. But there was a balsa wood buoy on the end of the line, so even if we couldn't hold the ray, we could follow it as long as we kept the buoy in sight.

After rushing for about a mile, the manta began to slow

down. We were able to catch up and seize the buoy with the end of the line. For about an hour the ray gave a fine display of his best tactics as he rushed this way and that to give us a hard time following him. Eventually we began to gain line a little and we decided to tire him out very quickly. This we did by stopping the motor so that two men could hold the line. But the manta seemed to be equal to our two men and forty-foot boat. I decided to try to increase our control over him by putting another dart in his left wing. We both pulled very hard against the fish's great power and at last we brought him within twenty feet of the boat—a good distance for a harpoon shot. Standing again in the prow, I let fly the dart, which again lodged where I wanted it in the left wing.

Then it happened. Maddened by the second dart, the manta took off at top speed with a terrific lunge. His sudden twist must have caused the line on the second harpoon to form a loop, for before I knew it, the line had got a turn on my leg. As the line burned into the flesh of my calf, I was being pulled with enormous force and nearly went overboard.

Guided by an overwhelming instinct of self-preservation, I flung out my arm and caught hold of the sampson post. My assistant threw himself on me and held me back with all his might. Miraculously the two of us managed to counterbalance the pull of the rope so that I was not jerked overboard. The rope left a scar ten inches round and a quarter of an inch deep, but the wound was much less painful to me than the thought of what might have happened if I had been dragged into the sea.

We could not stop to do much about my leg, however, for the manta was still demanding our attention. It took us four more hours to bring it within sight of the Seaquarium, and we did not attempt to boat it. We towed it behind the boat when its strength was exhausted, and then led it through a sluiceway into a viewing channel which is near the dock. There we removed the darts and allowed the manta to swim freely. We knew that it would not live long, for these rays hardly ever feed in captivity, but while it swam round, it was a notable specimen.

A smaller kind of ray which does thrive successfully in

captivity is the spotted whip, or leopard ray. As its name suggests, it is decorated with spots (white on a brown background), but the spots are on its back only; underneath it is white. The leopard ray could just as well be called a bat ray, however, because of its large wing-spread (about eight feet, maximum) and its upturned bat-like snout. Although the snout might be mistaken for a nose, it is actually a soft digging instrument with which the ray nuzzles the ocean bed and scrapes up molluscs or clams. The ray seizes its food in its mouth, which is on the underside of the snout, and grinds it up—hard shells and all—between two crusher plates in its jaws.

Another deceptive feature of the ray is its air holes, through which water is drawn in to be filtered out by the gills beneath. These huge holes could be mistaken for eyes, but they are really behind the eyes, which are on either side of the ray's head.

But most important for the fisherman to know about are the stingers at the base of the ray's very long, thin tail. There are about five of these bone-like barbs, each of which is nearly three inches long. When the ray presses them against an enemy, or when someone puts a hand or foot on them, they penetrate easily and poison the wound with a slime which coats them. They should be pulled out by continuing their thrust straight through, for if they are pulled back the way they entered, they will stick in the flesh and make the wound worse.

We catch the stinger-weaponed rays by putting out between two anchors a 700-foot net of wide nylon mesh. Along the top of the net are corks, and on the bottom are strips of lead, which weigh the net down so as to keep it vertical. When we put the net out, we anchor the large boat nearby and wait for a cork to bob down. This shows us that the ray has become entangled in the net, to which we hurry out for his capture in the small skiff.

Results are best when the tide is going out, for as the water becomes shallower, the ray leaves the bottom where he has been feeding and swims out to deeper water. At this time as many as two or three corks may bob down at once. We then bring the skiff nearby and cut the motor. Two of us lean over the side to pull the ray in while the third watches the motor.

Our first job is to remove the ray's dangerous stingers, for which purpose we carry a pair of pliers. To pull each stinger off is simple for us and painless for the ray, who is too busy trying to flop himself out of the boat to really notice the operation.

Once he is stinger-less, we rush him back to the live-well barge, put him on a net stretcher, and lift him out of the boat. This stretcher, slung between two poles, has an extra flap of net at one end so that when the ray is safely on, the flap can be thrown over him to prevent him slipping out. As soon as he is imprisoned in this way, he stops leaping and flapping his wings—as if he knew all was up. Once he has calmed down the ray can be very carefully lifted and guided by his air holes. He has no fins or other easily-grasped appendages.

But although he may give up struggling in the net, the ray does not take easily to captivity. In the live-well he will immediately—like the sharks—try to push the walls away from him. After he learns that they don't yield, he tries to find a way out by feeling them all over with his soft snout.

As soon as he is captured, the leopard ray's rich brown colour begins to fade, and by the time he is brought to the aquarium, he is a murky grey. Good living will partly restore the original colour, but he will never be quite as fine-looking as he was in the ocean. All fish, in fact, lose some of their colour in captivity; for this reason, when ichthyologists classify fish, they often list as two separate items their appearance before capture and the changed appearance shortly afterwards.

One of the most basic categories the ichthyologist uses to describe any sea-creature is its membership in the class of mammals or the class of fish. Mammals, as most people know, are distinguished mainly by the fact that they suckle their young. But it is not necessary to see an ocean creature with its young to tell whether or not it is a mammal. It is very easy to find out by looking at the tail, which on mammals is horizontal, and on fish, vertical.

Now the sharks, jewfish, and rays which I have been talking about are all fish. But the Seaquarium also collects such mammals as the manatee (sea cow) and the porpoise. The manatee is a huge, sluggish, grey-skinned creature, whose head, despite few whiskers and the absence of tusks, is a little like that of a walrus. On top of the manatee's head are two blow-holes with automatic lids which open as the manatee surfaces to breathe and close as it goes below.

Although the manatee is not particularly beautiful, it is said to have inspired the well-known tales about bewitching mermaids. Both the manatee and its Indian Ocean relative, the dugong, suckle their young, which are born alive, by holding them in their flippers. Since these flippers (short pectoral fins) are located where our arms would be, the nursing animal brings to mind a human mother holding a baby. The sailors of ancient times, who must have seen this phenomenon, probably brought back stories of strange beings, half feminine and—because of the manatee's huge, flat, horizontal tail—half fish.

The manatee is also associated—less romantically!—with the cow; it likes to "browse" on the plentiful vegetation of the brackish (half salt, half fresh) Florida inlets. This habit, plus the manatee's peaceful nature, explains why it is sometimes called a sea cow.

Because this interesting creature would make a fine exhibit for the Seaquarium, we were delighted one day to hear that a specimen had been spotted in an estuary about twenty-five miles away. We had to obtain a permit for its capture, because this now-rare animal, which used to be killed in large numbers for its very tasty meat, is protected by Florida state law.

We decided to capture the sea cow not by boat, but by truck, so that we could transport it to the aquarium more quickly. We knew that despite its sluggish nature, the animal could be a difficult opponent: it weighs about half a ton, has heavy, unyielding flesh, and is a very powerful swimmer. In preparation we loaded extra-heavy nets on the truck.

When three assistants and I arrived at the estuary, we decided to cut off the manatee's one possible exit to the sea

with a net. We would then try to close in on it and bind it
with ropes. But first we had to find it. In the dark water of
the estuary it was not easy to locate a large, dark object, and
we would have felt rather foolish simply peering into the
depths. Instead we waited for the manatee to surface and
breathe through its blowholes, as it must every five or ten
minutes.

When it did appear, there was no time to lose. An assistant
and I seized one end of the net and swam across the estuary
with it. But despite its size, the manatee was very nearly too
quick for us; we felt its tug on the net just as we were almost
across. To help us my other two assistants had to come into
the water with the other end of the net. The four of us were
able to wrap the manatee in it like a parcel of paper, and the
struggles of the frightened animal were an additional advantage, for as it thrashed about with its huge tail it got itself
even more entangled. Now we were able to tie heavy ropes
around it and drag it to the side of the estuary.

Before we had set off to capture the manatee, we had made
arrangements with a construction company to hire a large
derrick for lifting it out of the water. Now we quickly attached
the ropes which held the manatee to the derrick; it was
hoisted from the water, swung across to our truck, and lowered
on to several wet mattresses. (Creatures accustomed to the
swinging motions of water cannot travel on a flat, hard surface,
but mattresses are a good substitute.)

The manatee survived the journey very well indeed and
was soon swimming happily in her special tank at the Seaquarium. I am able to talk about her with the female pronoun
since Cleo, as she was named, triumphantly proved her sex
when she produced a baby Cleo in her tank five months later.

The two Cleos no longer inhabit the manatee pool, but two
other manatees do, and we have an unusual problem with
them. Since they are not constantly in motion, algae very
quickly grow on them; if they are left alone, they soon become
covered with a green slime—as often happens in their natural
state. To restore their hide to its original colour we give them
a good scrubbing every so often. The water in the pool is

lowered so that one of the attendants can stand in it; he takes a large scrubbing brush and rubs down the manatees' broad grey backs.

3

Unhappy Endings

MY job as a collector of live fish for aquaria and museums can be compared to that of a big-game hunter who stocks zoos. This job involves catching the right sort of specimen, capturing it in such a way as not to hurt it, and transporting it with care to wherever it is to be exhibited or studied.

Since all living creatures are unpredictable, and fish are no exception, I have to be prepared to deal with any specimen whenever and wherever it should turn up. And I also have to suffer some disappointments when the fish I have worked very hard to capture do not survive even the journey to the Seaquarium.

Several years ago, for instance, I made an unsuccessful attempt to collect a broadbill swordfish. Now swordfish are usually found in the North Atlantic during the summer—and this was July—but a broadbill swordfish is almost completely unheard of in Florida at any time of the year. What had caused this lone specimen to stray so far from its usual routes I do not know. At any rate I was informed by telephone that it was swimming round a lagoon off Fat Deer Key, about one hundred miles south of Miami. Even though I had just returned from an arduous three-week collecting trip in the Bahamas, I lost no time in getting together the heavy nylon nets I would need to capture the fish. Accompanied by the manager of the Seaquarium, I drove to the Key in a truck, as there was no time to go by sea.

(At this point I should make it clear that the swordfish is not to be confused with the sawfish; the resemblance is in the names only. The swordfish is sometimes as heavy as 16 hundredweight. Unlike the sawfish, which tends to remain at the bottom of the sea, it swims near the surface. It feeds on smaller fish and, as many of us know, is itself good eating.)

But to return to my story: when we reached the lagoon, we saw that a large crowd of spectators had gathered. Some of them persisted in throwing stones at the fish—a perversity for which I could see no reason.

The lagoon was open at the western end and closed on the other three sides. Because the opening was about five hundred feet wide, there was no doubt that the fish could get out if he wanted to. But some instinct must have told him that he ought to be going in a north-easterly direction to join his fellows in the North Atlantic; throughout the day he had never turned to the exit in the west, but had swum backwards and forwards along the eastern shore.

The wisest plan, we decided, would be to cut off the western retreat with a net, in case we should frighten the swordfish into turning round and escaping. We stretched the net from shore to shore and, in the boat we had borrowed from a motel owner on Fat Deer Key, advanced on the fish with another net. With this net we surrounded him. When he realized that he was penned in, he began to get restive.

Suddenly he lunged for the net at top speed and thrashed desperately about. This was what we had hoped for, because, as with the manatee, the net's tangles gave us something to grasp while we dealt with the slippery creature. We held him just long enough for me to slip a rope on his tail. Then we allowed him to swim free of the net, and he took some of the line with him. As he settled down to a steady pull against the rope, we imagined him swimming calmly in the Seaquarium tank.

But unexpectedly he turned wrong side up—a sign that he had given up hope and wanted to die. I didn't want this to happen if I could help it, so I jumped into the water and released the tail rope. Seizing his fins, I began to walk him round, forcing water through his gills, in the same way as we walk the sharks.

The water was chest-deep, and the going was hard, but I frantically continued until I was almost too exhausted to hold the fish, let alone walk him. But my efforts failed. The fish died in my arms.

I had another disappointment about three years ago, when I thought one of my dearest ambitions—capturing a whale for the Seaquarium—was about to be realized. With it the whale would bring problems—building a large enough tank, for example—but I knew that these problems had been solved in other sea aquaria, although their whales had not lived for long.

I have always wanted to take a whale when it is fairly young and small—about half a ton or so—so that I could watch its growth. But I couldn't order such things from nature, and when the opportunity to take a full-grown whale seemed to present itself, I had to grab it.

The specimen available was a pilot whale (also known as blackfish or caa'ing whale), which belongs to the family Globicephala, a word of Greek origin meaning "having a swelling forehead". The huge forehead which overshadows his mouth and dwarfs his eyes is one of the pilot whale's most obvious characteristics.

He is also known for a distressing habit of committing suicide. Tales throughout history have shown him suddenly coming into shallow water and going aground on beaches. In fact he gets the name "pilot" because when one of a school of whales decides he will run ashore, all the rest follow. There are no satisfactory explanations for this extraordinary action, although many have been attempted. Someone has suggested, for example, that the whales run ashore when they are chased by orcas, or killer whales—huge and terrifying monsters about whom I shall have more to say later on. But these orcas have very prominent dorsal fins, which can be seen from a long way off, and so far no one has reported seeing these fins near a school of pilot whales.

These schools, by the way, are very large. One numbering 1,540 is known to have run ashore off the Shetland Islands in 1845; every whale died or was killed. Not only the size of the group, but the bulk of the individual makes a school of pilot whales an impressive sight. These whales are sometimes as long as twenty-eight feet and as heavy as $2\frac{1}{2}$ tons.

At the time I was after a whale, a school of fifty or more had run ashore at Marathon, about one hundred miles from Miami. Having landed in water far too shallow to support them, the whales thrashed so vigorously that they filled the blowholes on top of their heads with sand and dirt and could not breathe. Some kindhearted people had thought to rescue them by tying ropes around their tails and towing them out to sea, but it was very disheartening to see that the whales turned right round and headed back for the shore.

When we were telephoned about this, we learned that although many whales had already died, there were some still alive which might easily be captured for the Seaquarium. We immediately loaded our truck with gear for securing the whale—nets and ropes, and slings in which to hoist it—and equipment for bringing it home in the truck—tubs for water to bathe it, blankets to keep it wet, and air mattresses to give it a smooth ride.

Driving as fast as we could, we came down the causeway towards Marathon at two o'clock in the morning. When we saw a great commotion in the water, we stopped the car and got out. With the aid of a strong flashlight we could see a whale nearly eighteen feet long, which was stuck in the mud; its back was well out of the water. As it tried to squirm free, it only made things worse. Entangling itself more with each effort, it made an unearthly sound through its blowhole, a sound which had all the tragic feeling of a creature in mortal danger, caught in the grips of something it could not understand. That sound, repeated throughout the blackness of the February night, still strikes terror into me whenever I recall it.

Full of pity I walked out to the trapped whale, but I immediately realized that we would be unable to help it. We would not be able to get the truck close enough to haul it out because a deep channel of water separated it from the road.

Farther along the causeway, on the bank at the far side of

the channel, we saw several other huge forms—also trapped and flailing in the mud. Then we saw several dead whales, obviously washed in on the tide and now left high and dry.

We went to see the friend who had telephoned us earlier, and he told us exactly where to find other whales which were still alive. In the middle of the night, followed everywhere by the mournful cry of the whales, we searched every spot our friend had suggested. But wherever we found a whale still alive and suitable for transportation it was lying on soft mud, where we could not bring up a truck—let alone a derrick which would enable us to hoist it.

The situation seemed hopeless until our friend remembered that one of the beached whales had been towed round to the marina dock—where of course it was still in deep water—and tied to a piling. In the darkness we drove round to the marina where we woke the sleepy proprietor and asked him for his whale. Not only was he willing to give it to us, but he also offered to lend us a motor boat and to help us lift the whale with an electric hoist he used for lifting boats. His help brought our party up to six (four had originally started, and my friend had joined us). But as we inspected the whale in the motor boat, we could guess that we would have to manœuvre more than twice our combined weight.

We towed the whale underneath the hoist, which had been swung out over the water. Leaning over the side of the boat, we managed to put one stretcher under him from each end and to tie him securely. Slowly and gently he was lifted out of the water and on to the air mattresses in the back of the truck. To keep his very sensitive skin from cracking he was draped in wet blankets, and to keep him from falling off the truck if he made a sudden movement, he was again tied securely.

Now we thanked our friends, jumped into the truck, and dashed for Miami as fast as we could safely and legally drive. Three of our party sat in front, and the fourth sat behind so that he could continually pour water over the whale's eyes and head.

All went well until we came within ten miles of the Sea-quarium, when our fourth man suddenly beamed a flashlight signal to the front. We stopped the truck and rushed to the whale, who was lying very still.

"He went into convulsions and died," his nurse said sadly.

We told the news to the crowd of reporters and photographers who were waiting for us at the Seaquarium.

But our work was not completely wasted, because we gave the whale's body to the University of Miami's Marine Laboratory, which is next door to the Seaquarium. The university scientists dissected it to try to find out what makes such whales commit suicide. But they did not discover anything, and although they have since dissected other whales, the exact reason has not yet been established.

Thinking back on our strenuous expedition, I reflected that although I have to seize every opportunity which arises, it is better to hunt a whale in the open sea than to haul him in from the beach. For it seems that the whale must in some way be unhealthy before he will run ashore, and only a healthy fish stands a chance of adapting to life in captivity.

For reasons of health, I think, we have had bad luck with an oversized creature called the mola mola, or ocean sunfish. This primitive fish, which belongs to the order of *Plectognathi*, should not be confused with the fresh-water sunfish small boys catch in inland ponds; it is a deep-water fish, which is often seen when it surfaces to lie on its side and sun itself. When fully grown it is more than eight feet long and weighs nearly a ton. Its mouth, which is incongruously tiny for its great bulk, looks as if it were divided into compartments because there is a single tooth in each jaw. Its flesh is so soft that if you were to hang the fish up and puncture it, most of this flesh would run out like unset jelly. But the mola mola is most easily recognized by its unusual shape. It looks as if it has no tail or body, as if some giant hand has beheaded it, leaving only the head to swim around.

It is easy enough to come upon one of these huge creatures and put a hook in its dorsal fin. We have done this and have brought the fish in by laying it on its side in the live-well. But no specimen has ever begun to eat.

A possible explanation for this was suggested when Craig

Phillips, the former curator of the Seaquarium, now curator of a national aquarium under construction in Washington, D.C., performed an autopsy on a mola mola and found it full of parasitic worms, which had eaten its internal organs. It may be that this fish is so easy to capture, despite its size, because it is a prey to these worms. Perhaps it is sickness which makes the fish rise from its normal depths for long periods and which weakens it so that, once at the surface, it puts up no resistance to capture.

Sickness was clearly responsible for the spiritless behaviour of the largest leopard ray we have ever had at the Seaquarium —an eight-foot $3\frac{1}{2}$ hundredweighter. It was caught while the Seaquarium divers, who feed the large fish in the main tank three or more times a day, were enjoying their lunch hour diving in the bay. As soon as they saw the ray swimming near the stanchions of a bridge, they seized it, took out its stings, and towed it with a rope to the Seaquarium dock, from which it was taken to the tank. It swam majestically for three days and then, without having eaten, sickened and died. The ray's size suggested that it was rather old, but old age alone could not have explained its easy submission to capture.

Like two other big fish, then—the whale and the mola mola —the ray was a disappointment. I have received great pleasure, on the other hand, from one of the tiniest fish in the Sea-quarium. Swimming in one of our smaller tanks is an exceed-ingly busy little fellow about an inch and a half long. All day long, and probably all night, too, he flutters his fins as he investigates the corals and shells which decorate the tank. His front half is a bright orange-yellow, and the rest of his body is a deep intense blue. His bright eye is encircled with a ring of blue, which makes him look as if he were wearing a monocle. This colourful creature, the only one of his kind in captivity, is known as the pigmy angelfish. His official name, *Centropyge argi*, is almost as long as he is!

It is the capture and preservation of such unusual fish which gives my job its sense of real adventure. Until recently diving equipment has not been well enough developed to allow much underwater exploration for specimens. Thus the main families of fish are very well known, but much detail remains to be filled in. A new sub-species, for instance, can be discovered. Or a fish may be known in either its young or adult form, but not in both forms; it is important for aquaria to find such a fish and watch its development. And it is sometimes possible to find an almost completely unknown specimen, as we did on the afternoon of June 6th, 1958, when we discovered the pigmy angelfish.

Four of us, including Craig Phillips, then curator at the Seaquarium, were collecting reef fish that afternoon on a reef a few miles south of Bimini in the Bahama Islands. I shall have more to say later about the means of collecting reef fish, but for the moment I will just mention that one of the collectors was skin-diving by the reef with an aqua-lung.

He went down not far from the *Sea Horse*, where the rest of us were digesting a well-earned lunch after a heavy morning's fishing. All of a sudden he came up and excitedly told us he had seen a fish he didn't recognize. We gave him a small net and he dived again.

He returned with a tiny fish, which he put in the live-well, where we could all get a good look at it. At first Phillips thought it was a damselfish, but when he noticed a "spine" (small spike) extending backwards from its gill-cover, he realized that the fish must belong to the angelfish family. Phillips told us in great excitement that this discovery was indeed rare, as such a miniature angelfish was thought to exist only in the Pacific and Indian Oceans. When my assistant told us that there were more angelfish below, we forgot everything else for the rest of the afternoon. We caught five more angelfish that afternoon, and two of my assistants caught six more two days later.

When we returned to the Seaquarium, Phillips telephoned an eminent ichthyologist at the Chicago Natural History Museum; he agreed with Phillips's identification of our discovery.

Phillips then told us that only two specimens of this fish had previously been known. One was taken off the Argus Reef in the Bermuda Islands in 1908. It was sent, preserved, to the Chicago museum, where unaccountably it must have been forgotten, for it was not described until 1951. The other specimen was found in 1952—in the stomach of a snapper caught off Yucatan. It was also sent to Chicago, and its identity was established by comparison with the earlier specimen.

To make absolutely sure we had identified our own fish correctly we borrowed the second specimen from Chicago to compare with ours. The comparison not only confirmed our identification, but showed that our fish were especially rare because they were in their young form.

We kept six of our eleven angelfish and distributed the others among museums and scientific institutions. Of our six, five mysteriously died shortly after they arrived. But the one survivor seems to be extremely happy and healthy, as he peers with his monocled eye into all the nooks of his tank. His cheerful colours are a daily reminder of the triumphs of my job.

4

Willow Poles and Buckets

THERE cannot be many men in this country—perhaps in the world—who follow my profession of bringing fish back alive. Perhaps such an unusual job should have an extraordinary beginning, but I'm afraid mine didn't. It seemed to develop naturally from my youthful love of fishing.

I was born in 1891 in the tiny country village of Lima, Pennsylvania. There were three of us in the family: my elder brother Herman, my younger brother Harold, and myself, separated by two-year intervals. My father was a builder by trade and a farmer when there was no building to be done. Life was hard for him, but occasionally he managed to go fishing in the local streams.

Perhaps I picked up the fishing fever from him. At any rate my earliest and proudest memory of the sport is catching a six-inch sunfish when I was eight years old. I caught it with a willow pole equipped with string and a hook and I can still remember the thrill of bringing home that lovely fish with the red breast. I suppose my family ate it, although I can't remember; in any case my mother was as happy about my success as I was and she never ceased to encourage me.

From that day on, it seems to me, I spent my young days exploring streams and creeks, armed with my willow pole. A little later I ventured farther afield and brought home a rock bass ten inches long. In my own estimation I was becoming an angling expert. I think that soon afterwards I was bringing home my catch not singly, but by strings; I was providing quite a feast for the Gray family.

Just after the turn of the century, the family moved to the

Catskill Mountains in New York for my mother's health. That countryside with its cascading streams and quiet ponds seemed like paradise to my brothers and me, and we fished as if life consisted of nothing else. For my first Christmas in the Catskills, my mother gave me a real fishing rod of split bamboo, with a reel and line. The rod may not have taken any fish which would win prizes for size, but it was used enough to merit an award for long service.

My brothers and I used to ramble for a whole day at a time. Herman, naturally, was in charge of the party, and Harold, since he had not yet graduated to a rod of his own, came along to carry the fish. I think we must have fished every stream within a day's walk of our home. Because we felt that the farther we walked the better the fishing would be, we sometimes walked a great deal more than we fished, but we were young enough not to notice.

Within a year our home territory was so familiar that we were glad our family was moving again. This time we were going to Ocean Grove, New Jersey—to the sea. Visions of enormous and plentiful salt-water fish arose before our eyes. Fresh-water fish are good sport and good eating, but what delights were now to reveal themselves to us!

We were not disappointed in our new environment, for we could explore not only the seashore, but numerous bays and inlets, and such rivers as Shark River were within two hours' walking distance. We fished from piers and jetties, we dug clams, we caught crabs. I must confess that I played truant to go fishing more than I now think was wise.

We learned to recognize the crustacea (hard-shelled water creatures) which abounded in the mud flats, to know that the flounders which lay on the bottom near the rocks would bite best on live killifish, and that weakfish could only be caught with shedder crabs. As yet our angling ambitions were severely limited: a common skate was a deep-sea monster to us, and the sight of one brought to mind sea serpents and strange tales. But the smaller creatures were all in our kingdom and our natural prey.

Besides learning what we could by ourselves, we also

watched our elders. At certain times of the year when the striped bass were running close to the shore, many anglers with long surf-casting rods would come to the beach. They would stand in the surf, using what to us seemed such luxurious equipment, and they scorned all fish except the "stripes", or striped bass. We all hung around them, watching in awe and admiration, but we must have absorbed a lot of information without knowing it. Our heroes allowed us to dig blood worms and to gather shedder crabs and sea clams for them in exchange for the privilege of watching them fish. Their pleasure can hardly have been greater than ours when a striper, often more than two feet long and weighing nearly fifty pounds, was landed.

So far I had exclusively been a sports fisherman, but it was during this period at Ocean Grove that a new element entered my life. I must have been about thirteen when I was taken to the John Wanamaker store in Philadelphia. Naturally I wandered to the aquarium department. It was not strange that Wanamaker should have such a department, for at the beginning of the century many homes had in the front parlour a small round bowl containing a goldfish or two. More elaborate homes had large rectangular aquaria equipped with flowing water, aquatic plants, miniature castles under water, electric lights, and assorted tiny fish.

But although fish were in fashion then, it must have been a slack period at Wanamaker's, for I remember that I got into conversation with the manager of the department. He proudly showed me a tank containing very rare and expensive fish, all about two inches long. I recognized the fish at once, but said nothing. The manager told me the fish were members of a species called *Mesogonistus chaetodon*, a name which, as in the case of the pigmy angelfish, was longer than the fish themselves.

I felt that people must be paying for the name rather than for the fish, for I knew it as a black-banded sunfish—one of the family which began my angling career and which was very commonly found in fresh-water streams and ponds near my New Jersey home. However, if people were willing to pay for the fish and its name, I could very easily oblige them and do myself some good as well.

"How much would you pay for each of these fish if I brought them to you?" I asked politely.

"Twenty-five cents each," he replied. Anyone remembering what twenty-five cents was worth in 1904 will understand what dreams of wealth unfolded before my mind's eye.

That very afternoon I arranged with the manager to buy black-banded sunfish from me when he had orders for them. When I had accumulated orders into the hundreds—once or twice a week—I would take a hand-net and a bucket into the swamps and streams around my home. Then I would bring my catch into Philadelphia in a bucket or tub. To get to the aquarium department I suppose I must have entered Wanamaker's by a back entrance, for I cannot imagine carrying a dripping bucket through all the other departments!

Thus began my professional career. I made a great deal of pocket money, and later in my life I was to fill a hungry hiatus in the same way.

Since those early days, my life has always been connected with fish and the sea. But until the end of World War II, I had two separate, though parallel, interests: sports or commercial fishing, and collecting. I made my living catching and killing fish, both for sport and for food, but always at the back of my mind was a desire to see fish swimming happily in natural surroundings—and to let other people see them too. Whenever I could, I collected fish instead of killing them. But it was not until the Seaquarium was opened that I could devote myself entirely to showing other people the fish I have known all my life. The Seaquarium is, in a very real sense, the crown of a life's work.

While I was first learning the tricks of the collecting trade, my brother Herman turned sixteen and went to work. As you might expect, he wanted to be near only one place—the sea. He became a mate on one of the fishing skiffs which put out from Ocean Grove, and I spent a great deal of time helping him.

In those days, before outboard motors and self-starters were known, sea skiffs were launched from the beach. This was a hazardous undertaking because of the huge breakers, which made the coast white with surf.

The skiff on which Herman worked used to be kept ready for launching on wooden rollers at the beach. When it was launched, a man would be stationed by its inboard motor; he would be ready to start up as soon as the boat hit the water. To steer the boat over the breakers the mate would be ready at the oars. A band of launchers, of which I was one, was usually on hand to assist; we would wait anxiously for a "slatch" between the breakers. The breakers rolled in sets of three, and the slatch was the division between the sets.

The captain, at the motor, would call, "O.K. boys, watch for the next slatch and shoot her out!"

As the slatch came, we would all push the boat out and jump in, hoping that the mate on the oars would keep her straight until she got beyond the line of breakers. If he didn't she would very likely capsize.

The boat would stay out all day, squidding or trolling for bluefish and bonito in the summer, and trawling or fishing with a hand-line for cod during the winter. Then in the evening, with the boat full of fish, we would head for our landing.

In order to avoid the breakers again, the boat had to be rolled up on to its rollers as quickly as possible. At the moment the prow touched the shore, we jumped out and pulled the boat up by means of a winch or turnstile. It was dramatic and exciting, but very serious, for an upset boat would mean a lost catch.

Since such operations interested me far more than studying, I was all impatience for the time I could devote my days to fishing. I didn't have long to wait, for when I turned sixteen, I left school and became Herman's mate (he had his own boat by now). I worked for him for two or three years, until I got my own boat, the *Amberjack*. Now I myself was an employer in a small way, since I had a mate working for me, but our venture was actually a co-operative one; if we both did well, both of us became briefly rich, and if we caught nothing, neither of us got paid.

Our life was, I realize now, a hard one. We fished every day it was possible to go out—mostly for bluefish and bonito; the hours were often very long, and the weight of the fish was back-breaking. When we returned at night, we sold our catch —if there was any—to a buyer whose truck was waiting at the shore to take it to market. On a good day we would have five or six hundredweight of fish to sell him.

But our work didn't seem hard to me at the time; fishing had always been pleasure and it still was. When a day without a catch came along, there would be disappointment, but it was not tragedy. A true fisherman is somehow equipped by nature to take troubles in his stride. For fishing has been the same since the beginning of time. If today is a bad day, perhaps tomorrow will be a good one, and if not tomorrow, the next day.

Besides the occasional lack of fish, however, we did have other trials. Around July and August we encountered huge fish we called horse-mackerel, which played havoc with our tackle. When we were out for bluefish, our bread and butter in late summer, each of us, captain and mate, looked after two lines. I held the tiller with one hand and watched two lines on the starboard side, while the mate watched two on the port side. We set up the oars as outriggers on which to suspend the lines, so that they would not foul each other. When we ran into a school of horse-mackerel, we would feel a sudden jolt as if we had struck some underwater obstacle. What happened was that the great fish had lunged for each of the four lures at the same time; they had enough force to pull the boat to a standstill, break the lines, and sometimes the oars.

This happened again and again. Every time we went out with new tackle, we came back with half the lines and a broken oar or two. We tried substituting the heaviest possible lines for our normal 60 thread, but the mackerel broke that too. Some of our fellow fishermen tried harpooning them, but although they got a few, they didn't discourage the rest. Worse yet, the successful fishermen were left with a 1 to $1\frac{1}{2}$ hundredweight fish they could not profitably dispose of. No one had yet thought of these tuna as food fish, so they had no market value.

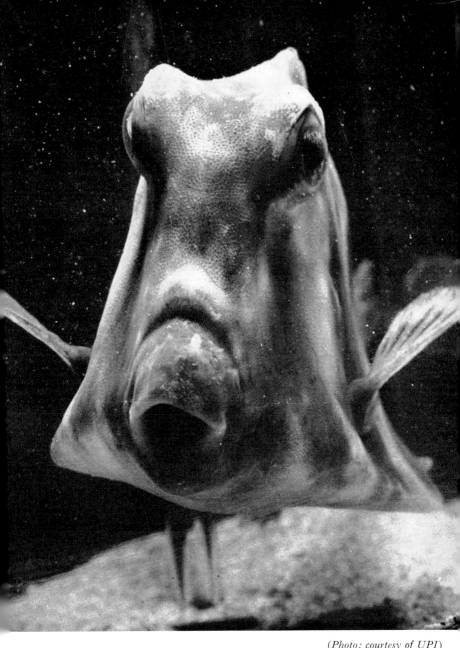

At the Seaquarium: the rare trunkfish.

(*Photo: courtesy the Seaquarium*)

(*above*) Three of the Seaquarium's collecting boats. The live-well barge is lashed to the cabin cruiser at the left; to the right is one of our skiffs.

(*below*) Another rare fish, the red hind.

(*above*) In the live-well of the Sea Cow I arrange tiger sharks to make room for others still on the line.

(*below*) A hooked shark.

This porpoise on a mattress is ready for its journey to the Seaquarium. To prevent fever after capture, it must be kept wet until it is hoisted into our main tank.

(*Photos: courtesy the Seaquarium*)

(*above*) The submarine crew can hoist this whale only half-way because of its weight.

(*below*) Sharks which have just been caught are transported from the live-well to the holding tanks on a stretcher.

(*Photo: courtesy the Seaquarium*)

A pilot whale being hoisted in a sling towards the truck. Notice its
tongue and heavy forehead.

(*above and below*) Traps for collecting reef fish.

(*right*) I am mending a net used for catching porpoises.

(*above*)   Green turtles hatch from perfectly spherical eggs.

(*below*)   Baby green turtles in the water.

For it turned out that our horse-mackerel were in fact bluefin tuna, destined to develop not only into one of the most widely known food fish, but into the objects of great sport for fishermen in the 1930s and 1940s.

They were no sport for us. Bluefish at that time brought only four cents a pound—compared with seventy or eighty cents now!—and the continual replacement of tackle was a drain on our income.

At this time I began to read exciting newspaper stories about a group of anglers who were catching the big tuna for sport off the California coast. I learned that the first tuna in the world had been taken off Avalon, on Catalina Island, in the 1890s, and the first Tuna Club in the world had been organized at Catalina in 1898. But what interested me particularly about the articles was their description of West Coast anglers using rod and reel. The stories concentrated not on the ordeal of the fish, but on the endurance tests of the fishermen. This emphasis I well understood from my own experience, but the use of rod and reel for such big fish was new to me. During the Catalina club's first season the record catch had weighed 1½ hundredweight—an amazing performance for the tackle which was used at that time.

If tuna were being caught this way on the West Coast, I thought, what about the New Jersey coast? After all, we had seen plenty of tuna here. I wrote an article on the possibilities of New Jersey tuna fishing and sent it to the *Forest and Stream* magazine, a forerunner of the present *Field and Stream*.

The publication of the article, a great boost to my youthful pride, brought me a large number of letters from sports fishermen who were willing to risk themselves and their tackle against the Atlantic Coast tuna. Before I really knew what I was in for, I agreed to take some of these men out with me on a charter basis. The excursion was likely to be more profitable for me than a commercial trip, for whether we caught anything or not, I was to be paid in advance for my services.

Since most of the tuna I had seen off Ocean Grove would weigh at least three or four hundredweight, I hadn't the least idea how we would bring one to boat if we ever got that far.

4

But I felt sure I'd find out, and the anglers displayed the same cheerful ignorance.

Hooking tuna proved to be no problem at all. They were plentiful and hungry. We hooked them by trolling the bait—allowing the baited lines to follow the boat—and chumming, throwing handfuls of bait in its wake. Chumming attracted the fish to the boat, and while they were there, they were more than likely to pick up a piece of bait with a hook in it.

But then came the problem. Our tackle was just not up to the strain of playing a 3-hundredweight tuna swimming away from us at top speed. The angler at that time used a 60 reel, with three or four hundred yards of 21 thread line at 60-pound test, and the only braking power on the reel was his thumb enclosed in a leather case. Later refinements such as star drags, gimbel rod butt sockets, and nylon thread line were unknown. Nor was there a swivel chair and harness; standing in the boat and holding his rod in a leather socket-belt strapped round his waist, the fisherman was often in danger of losing his balance and falling overboard.

When the tuna struck our bait, the fight was often all over before we knew it had begun, for he either took all the line off the reel, or broke the rod and line at one crack. Even if our tackle had been able to hold him, we would have been in trouble; our boat went seven miles an hour, and tuna could travel at least twice as fast.

We made twenty trips that season without boating a single tuna. Eventually we did manage to bring a few to shore, but none weighed more than one hundredweight. The chief benefit of our frustrating experiences was their contribution to the development of fishing tackle. Necessity is of course the mother of invention, and it was not long before invention caught up with the tuna.

After my disappointments I gave up the business of charter boat fishing, for the guaranteed income was not worth the frustration. But I hadn't finished with tuna. They and I were to have many more battles before I would finally come to grips with them thirty years later.

5

First Sight of Florida

I WAS so downhearted about my experiences with tuna in the summer of 1909, that I was glad to be diverted by ideas for a new enterprise. During the previous winter several of our fishing friends had taken their boats and equipment to the lower east coast of Florida. Instead of fishing for cod, as we did off New Jersey in the winter, they netted Spanish mackerel and bluefish. There was a local market for their catch, they told us, as well as the pleasures of warm sunshine, flowers, and coconuts.

Because I was so discouraged at the time, and because we liked the prospect of winter fishing without ice-coated lines and frostbitten fingers, my brother Herman and I decided to try Florida for one winter. Herman and I and our respective mates brought our equipment to Jupiter Inlet, which ran from the town of Jupiter to the coast, about twenty miles north of Palm Beach. Starting from scratch, we built ourselves a small house with a palmetto thatched roof, a cook house and a bunk house. Here we lived very comfortably in the Florida sunshine.

Since the area around Jupiter Inlet was known for its abundance of mackerel, bluefish, and the beautiful silvery pompano, a wholesale fish company had opened a receiving station in Jupiter. We moved up and down the coast following the runs of fish and brought our catch back to Jupiter to sell it.

As a result of that winter, we decided that in the future we would spend the summers in New Jersey and the winters in Florida. This we did for a number of years, even after I married in 1912.

In Florida there was again time to continue my collecting interests. When the weather was too rough for us to go out, or when the fish were not easily found near the shore, we would explore the inland waters, the jungles and everglades. I spent many happy days learning about the fish which lived in fresh and brackish water and I was constantly amazed at their great variety. I seemed continually to be finding a fish which I had never seen before.

In the inland fresh water I found great quantities of black *Gambusia* and black *Mollienisia*—kinds of dwarf minnows which in the aquarium markets of the North were considered very rare. Naturally they were very expensive there.

I contacted my old buyers, such as the manager of the, aquarium department at John Wanamaker's in Philadelphia and soon had many orders for these tiny fish. I would net them from their inlets and creeks by the pailful and send them to northern pet shops in large tin containers by rail. Before long, other fishermen discovered my occupation, and all too soon the supply caught up with the demand. For them, however, catching minnows was only a reasonably easy way to make money; for me it was another step forward in my development as a collector.

After about five years of alternating between New Jersey and Florida, I moved to Trenton, New Jersey, to become a wholesale and retail fish merchant. I had an establishment at the corner of Clinton St. and High St., to which I devoted myself almost entirely. Anything to do with fish requires patience and shrewdness, for you cannot control your raw material; nature does that.

I thought a great deal about Florida at this time and even spent one winter—1920 I think—chasing bluefish at Fernandina on the extreme northern coast. I had heard that bluefish were very plentiful there, but they didn't run for us.

We turned instead to shrimp, which were just becoming popular as food. I found that there was no way to bring in large numbers of them, so with the pioneering instinct which must be in my blood, I decided to try trawling for them with a large net. The net had to be made first, and because this would have been very expensive to buy, four of us made one ourselves. We operated it at a great profit for a while, and even began to make trawl nets and sell them to our fellow fishermen. But the idea of trawling for shrimp was too good to remain ours for long, and within two months there were dozens of shrimp trawls operating from Fernandina. The markets were soon overloaded, the price dropped rapidly, and the bottom fell out of shrimping.

I went back to New Jersey, but the pull of Florida was too strong. In 1924 my wife and I moved to West Palm Beach, where we were to spend the next eighteen years.

At that time, when yachting was in its heyday, there were many huge and luxurious yachts anchored at West Palm Beach. Some of them were appointed as comfortably as ocean-going liners; they were ideal locations for the gay parties of the twenties, the era of short skirts and long cigarette-holders.

Magnificent as these yachts were, they presented a problem: they had to be re-fuelled by the extremely arduous method of bringing petrol tanks in small boats from the docks. There were no petrol pumps on the docks in those days, and even if there had been, many of the yachts would have drawn too much water to come alongside the docks. Clearly there was a need for some convenient way of re-fuelling the yachts as they lay at anchor in the harbour.

An enterprising oil company had the right idea, and my brother Herman and I carried it out. The company purchased an old Mississippi riverboat, which it brought round the tip of Florida and up the coast to West Palm Beach, where it was moored in Lake Worth. From the outside it looked like a set from "Showboat", but inside it had petrol tanks which could hold up to 15,000 gallons of fuel. Herman and I added more tanks and stocked oil, water, food, and yacht supplies; we were now set up as a floating garage. Sometimes as many as six yachts at once could be seen re-fuelling around our barge, which must have looked like a sow feeding piglets!

Because our barge was so big it was as much of a problem to refill our own tanks as it was to re-fuel the yachts, but we solved that problem by running the barge under a railway bridge and piping petrol and oil directly from the tanks in the railway trucks above.

A picture of the barge was published in the local paper, where it was described as "probably the only one of its kind in the world". It could easily be seen by yachts which entered the lake, for not only was its shape extremely distinctive, but it was covered with enormous signs screaming "PETROL" and "OIL".

These were the days of prohibition, and Florida was a very convenient place for obtaining illicit liquor from the Bahama Islands, which of course are British and were therefore "wet". Many of the yachts we re-fuelled carried cargoes of illegal whisky, either to be distributed in the innumerable concealed ways which people thought up at that time, or to be enjoyed on board during the riotous parties for which the era was famous. We, of course, knew nothing of any such activities; our job was to fill the tanks of the yachts with petrol, and we did so. But the feeling of excitement was there.

Because Herman and I ran the barge jointly, we had plenty of opportunity to make other expeditions; each of us could leave the other in charge. Herman began to take out charter boat parties for sports fishing, while I continued my explorations for fish I could collect.

I started going farther afield than the inlets and rivers of Florida. In numerous trips to the Florida Keys and the Bahama Islands I discovered with delight the habits of their native fish.

Warmed by the Gulf Stream, the Bahamas and the southern part of Florida are tropical. The temperature of their water, rarely under seventy degrees, is usually about seventy-eight degrees; this enables the corals, tiny animals which work for thousands of years, to build their brightly coloured underwater reefs. The curving formations and innumerable indents of these reefs provide homes for hundreds of small fish. Any animal is equipped by nature to preserve itself against enemies, and the small reef fish are specifically protected by bright colouring that blends with their background. (Fish in northern waters, on the other hand, tend to look grey and sombre to match the drab-coloured ocean and ocean bottom.)

I collected the fish which I discovered for aquaria and pet shops and also began to sell to biological supply houses. A few firms in large cities, such as New York and Chicago, specialize in supplying schools and colleges with the specimens they require for teaching biology, zoology, and even the specialized subject of ichthyology (study of fish). The companies send out lists of their requirements, which give the prices they will pay for specimens—usually ordered by the hundred or the thousand. The order might be for a hundred jellyfish or starfish; for Portuguese men-o'-war (which, by the way, can leave a very nasty sting) or for a thousand sea snails. I would take the lists, tell the companies what I could get for them, and go off on the hunt. Since the specimens had to be preserved in alcohol, or a similar solution, I did not have my usual problem of bringing them back alive.

Museums also ordered a certain number of specimens from me, and in the course of time I came to know many of the reefs around Bimini and the other Bahamas like the back of my own hand. This knowledge was later to prove invaluable when I had to stock large salt-water aquaria.

But meanwhile I had plenty of time for sports fishing, as well as for fishing on order. I took hundreds of exciting expeditions to go after the great game fishes: tarpon, bonefish, barracuda, and—particularly—sailfish.

The sailfish is related to the marlin made immortal in Ernest Hemingway's *The Old Man and the Sea*. Its resemblance to the marlin is noticeable in the protrusion of its upper jaw or beak beyond the lower one to make a spike. The bony and rough-surfaced spike can do considerable damage to anything which gets in its way.

As it characteristically leaps from the water—in pursuit, perhaps, of the flying fish which make up part of its diet—the sailfish is seen to be grey-blue with a silver sheen. It spreads the large sail-like fin on its back to help it control its direction when it breaks through the surface. This fin, plus two other fins on its sides, fold into the fish's body when it is under water.

Because of its great speed, made possible by its streamlined shape and its very large tail, and because, when it is taken, it makes every possible leap and turn and rush to get away from the line, the sailfish is a magnificent sporting fish. I have a great respect for it as a fighter and an opponent.

It's a tough fish to catch for still another reason: it only takes bait which looks alive. The best way to deceive it is to cut a strip of flesh from the belly of a mullet, kingfish, or some other bait fish, and to fix this strip to the hook so that it wiggles.

For years I fished for sailfish whenever I had spare time. But although I had taken some large ones, I had never qualified for the diamond button awarded by the Sailfish Club of Florida for a fish over eight feet in length caught with light tackle. Of course I couldn't wait to get the button.

One day in March, 1928, when I was free to spend an afternoon sports fishing, a friend of mine suggested an expedition for sailfish. We set off in his boat from the Sailfish Club at Palm Beach and began trolling just off the shore. My friend preferred to try his luck with a whole mullet, but I stuck to my knowledge of marine psychology and used strips of mullet from the belly. After trolling along the shore, we went out slowly to the Gulf Stream, where sailfish were frequently found. But apparently there were none this afternoon, for the numerous boats we saw were not flying the pennant which means that such a fish has been taken. So we went south along the edge of the Stream.

At first this didn't seem like a very good idea, for we ran right into a school of sharks which took our bait and broke our lines. We turned back towards the shore at full speed and did not let our lines out again until we were fairly sure we had evaded the sharks. But when a huge dark fish began to follow my line, my heart sank. The sharks were back. Watching the fish follow the bait, I began to reel in the lines as fast as I could. As he came closer to the surface, I suddenly thought that he might not be a shark. When he lunged at the bait, I knew he wasn't; he was an enormous, beautiful, silver-grey sailfish!

Even while my heart pounded excitedly, I managed to throw the brake off the reel as the fish slashed at the bait. This let out more line so that the bait could remain close to the fish. My relief knew no bounds when the fish seized the bait and the line tightened.

With the hook in his mouth the fish hesitated. Then, not quite sure that he had *really* been hooked, he started away in his equivalent of low gear. I let him have the line for a few moments and then jammed it taut. As I felt the fish's weight, the hook set securely in his mouth, and he knew he was caught. Now he plunged away with all the speed in him.

My reel unwound so fast that it made a screeching noise as the thread paid out against the pressure of the drag on it. When the fish had two hundred yards of line, he suddenly leaped from the water in his characteristic way. We drew our breath at his tremendous size and beauty; if we could beat him, we would have the diamond button.

Several times he leaped, each time seeming to be suspended for a moment in mid-air. Shaking his head furiously, skidding around on his tail, and thrusting his spear out of water as if to strike, he tried to free himself from the line. With each new trick he changed direction, and each time he took a little more line. I began to worry that there would not be enough for him.

When he turned towards the boat and seemed to slacken speed, I thought I had won—and very easily too. I pulled on the line and slowly reeled it in until the fish was within fifty yards of the boat.

But I was wrong. With a renewed burst of energy my opponent suddenly broke water in the first of another series of breath-taking leaps. When he finished the last of these leaps, he took off again for more than two hundred yards. In the midst of his run he sounded (that is, dived right down) quite deeply, apparently gaining spring for another great leap. He repeated this run and spring again and again—sounding and leaping, sounding and leaping, until I thought my rod and reel would never stand the strain.

After playing him for an hour, I managed to bring him near the boat on three different occasions, but he always dashed off again. From somewhere in his body or spirit, he summoned up fresh reserves of energy. Again and again I felt sure that my reel would not have enough thread on it.

But even his great resources had to come to an end, and finally I began to gain on him. Slowly I managed to reel in the line and bring the exhausted fish nearer the boat. My arms ached so much that, when he was finally taken, I could not help to bring him aboard. My friend put on gloves, grabbed the fish's spear, and hauled him over the gunwale.

To our surprise he was not yet dead. Before they are boated, game fish often yield from sheer exhaustion, but this one was extraordinarily strong. To stretch him out on the floor and measure him we had to hold him down. We were delighted to find that his length overlapped the eight-foot mark on the floor of the boat.

I relaxed in the fishing chair and enjoyed the superb feeling of an ambition fulfilled. My friend hoisted the pennant to show that a sailfish had been caught, and we returned to the Sailfish Club in triumph.

When we brought our prize into the club to measure and weigh it, it was still alive and still willing to put up a fight. Its full length was 8 feet 2½ inches, and it won for me not only a diamond button, but also a special trophy for the largest sailfish of that year.

Three years later I was to take the world's record sailfish, but in a different place and under very different conditions.

6

The White Shadow

WHILE I was collecting fish or catching them for sport, my brother Herman looked after the barge. When I looked after the barge, he took out fishermen in his boat on a charter basis—often wealthy and distinguished people. Among his clients was George Vanderbilt, son of the late Alfred Gwynne Vanderbilt. He was then a very young man, but he had already developed a great interest in fish and wildlife. He had his own museum and later on he performed valuable collecting services for the Academy of Natural Sciences in Philadelphia.

In 1931 Vanderbilt thought he would like to pursue his hobbies farther afield. He organized an expedition which had a number of aims. Chief among them was the shooting of a three-reel film about deep-sea fishing off Panama. To shoot the film, which was to be called *Devil's Playground*, he took along the well-known cameraman Paul Burress. Herman was hired as captain of Vanderbilt's yacht, *White Shadow*; I was fishing director and collector of the specimens that Vanderbilt wanted for his museum. Herman's first mate, Harold Jensen, also came with us.

We set off on June 9, 1931, from Palm Beach and boarded the *White Shadow* at Cristobal in the Canal Zone. We went through the Canal to the Pearl Islands on its Pacific side, cruised along the coast of northern Panama to the island of Coiba, and returned through the Canal to the Caribbean. There we visited the San Blas Indians, who live on the Panama coast south of the Canal. On our way home we called at Havana, Cuba, where the large menagerie we brought with us attracted much newspaper attention.

Naturally the trip was full of incidents, but among the first and most exciting was the capture of a thirty-five-foot whale of the finback species, which we discovered one morning off the Pearl Islands. Vanderbilt, Herman, and I fought the creature all day, while Burress took pictures as if his life depended on it. We harpooned the whale frequently, but like all the members of Moby Dick's tribe, it took a great deal of punishment. It was late in the afternoon before we killed it, but Burress wanted still more pictures.

He particularly wanted to photograph the whale in its entirety, but we could imagine no way of making this possible. There was in the area, however, a fleet of U.S. submarines, whose crews were watching our performance with great interest. When the whale was dead, we approached one of the submarine tenders and asked if we might use its hoisting apparatus to lift the whale clear of the water. The crew was willing to help us and fixed the whale to the hoist by a sling round its tail. But because the whale weighed five or six tons, it could only be lifted out of the water half-way. To heave it up any higher would have damaged the hoisting apparatus. Burress was therefore forced to be satisfied with that, and we thanked the crew of the submarine tender for its help. By then it had grown too dark to shoot any more pictures, so we decided to tie up the whale in a quiet cove for the night and come back next morning. We towed it, since of course there was no other way to convey it, and tied it with ropes to trees on the shore.

Next morning we were up early, as always on these expeditions. In tropical islands the dawn is so beautiful that you feel you don't want to miss a single minute. On all expeditions I have taken everyone has returned in good health except for one thing—a need for a good night's sleep. At any rate, when we got to the cove and to our whale, we were horrified at what we saw. During the night a pack of sharks had smelled the whale and come from miles around to slash away at the flesh until there was almost nothing left but the skeleton. The water nearby, shallow as it was, was still full of the thrashing sharks, fighting for the whale's remains.

Since we could take no more pictures of the whale, we decided to get pictures of sharks—and to get our revenge on them at the same time. Perhaps it is not very honourable to wreak vengeance on creatures which, after all, are only following their natural instinct, but the sight of their carnage was too much. To us the sharks seemed calculatedly evil.

My brother attached a shark hook to a very heavy rope line, baited the hook with whale meat, and ran into the sea as close to the sharks as he dared. He threw the bait into their midst, and when one shark took it, he pulled the line and ran back to the beach. The rest of us seized the line and dragged in the shark, while Burress went on taking pictures. We repeated this manœuvre until the beaches were strewn with stranded sharks. Then we left them.

On the same islands where we had caught the whale we found green turtles in abundance. We enjoyed many a meal of their very tasty flesh and were able to get pictures of each stage of their lives—probably the first time their complete life cycle was captured on film.

These great unwieldy creatures are found in almost all warm oceans of the world, but they come out of the water to lay their eggs. During the laying season at full moon the female crawls as far up the shore as she can to get beyond high water mark. There she scoops out a hole about eighteen inches deep in the sand, in which she deposits her eggs. As many as two hundred of these eggs, which are as perfectly spherical as a ping-pong ball, can be laid at once. Using her large flipper the female covers the eggs so that no trace of them remains and returns to the ocean. The distinctive trail left by her flippers and the edge of her shell is the clue for those in search of a good meal.

After about six weeks of incubation by the heat of the sand, the eggs break and the baby turtles hatch out. By some instinct they know exactly which way to turn to reach the sea, and they scramble for it as soon as they are free of their shells. On the way they are an easy target for sea birds and predatory animals; probably not even half of a brood reaches the ocean. Once there the brood is subject to further depredation by large fish, as well as by more sea birds, who swoop near the surface and seize the babies from above. If they do manage to survive all these hazards—including human beings in search of a gourmet dish—turtles live on in the sea, slowly gaining a hard shell and a great deal of weight. They grow so gradually that it takes from eight to ten years for them to attain a weight of 1 hundredweight.

While we were taking pictures of their life cycle, we were also putting on film some exciting sports fishing dramas. Since the actors in a film about deep-sea fishing cannot be told to repeat their scenes, we had to be prepared to shoot whenever anything noteworthy happened. It was while we were filming one of these spontaneous scenes that I landed the world's record sailfish single-handed and, literally, very nearly with one hand.

Burress wanted as many pictures of leaping sailfish as possible, so that he could cut his film footage and preserve only the best ones. He frequently asked me to troll for sailfish and, whenever I hooked one, to play it until he got the shots he wanted. Then I would release it—a humane way of accomplishing our purpose without wasting fish needlessly.

On one particular morning he and I set off alone in a small fishing boat with an inboard motor. We chugged along very happily for a while, taking a few good-sized sailfish and then releasing them again, as we had planned. The waters around the Pearl Islands were full of fish, and it was not difficult to get them to bite.

Suddenly I hooked something enormous. I could tell by its weight that it was extra-large, but when it finally broke water and leaped, I knew it was the biggest sailfish I had ever seen. At once my plans changed: I wanted to boat the fish and take it back to claim the world's record, as I thought it would easily beat all others.

Now to play and boat a fish of that size you really need at least two pairs of hands, and preferably three, but the other pair of hands in the boat was eagerly turning the camera. Burress realized the size of the fish and the drama of the moment, but he was so intent on immortalizing it that he never dreamed of helping me.

For the next half hour I was—almost literally—a man torn in two; I had to hold the helm and control the motor with one hand and play the fish with the other. The fish gave a performance of such brilliant leaps and runs that even Burress was satisfied, but I was nearly frantic. I kept calling to Burress to take over the controls, but oblivious to everything except his camera, he only shouted for me to turn the boat round so that he could get a shot without the glare of the sun on the sea.

With one hand I played the fish, giving him line to leap on and then trying to pull him in a little. At last, after many long rushes and spectacular leaps, he began to lose strength, and I managed to pull him towards the boat.

Then I was presented with a problem, for I had only one pair of hands to lift him over the gunwale. I shut off the motor, managed to tug on a pair of gloves, and grabbed him by the bill. I pulled most of him over the side, and then the two of us went into a sort of see-saw game, as I pulled one way and he fought to go back the other. I don't know how long the struggle went on, but all the while Burress was taking pictures, a large proportion of which showed my seat as I leaned over the side.

Eventually I won, and laid the sailfish on the bottom of the boat. Then Burress, completely exhausted, did help me a little; he sat on the fish beside me and told me what a "terrific show" I had managed for the camera!

The fish turned out to be a monster—10 feet $8\frac{1}{4}$ inches long, and weighing $1\frac{1}{2}$ hundredweight. When we got it back to the *White Shadow*, we skinned it and later sent the skin to a taxidermist, who mounted it. My record was later broken, but the fish I caught with practically one hand remained the world's largest for quite a number of years.

If the fishing in the Pearl Islands was excellent, what we found as we went farther up the Pacific coast of Panama was paradise. In July we passed the island of Coiba and came upon a group of enchantingly beautiful islets. We decided to explore the waters around them to see if they would live up to the promise of the land.

We picked our way into a bay on the island of Secas and

let down the anchor into six fathoms of water so clear that we could see it resting on the bottom. This clarity was all the more remarkable because we were near the shore, where the water is often more cloudy than it is farther out. Sloping to the water's edge was a steep mountain covered with dense tropical plants and trees. From the foliage we heard the squawks of variously coloured parrots, obviously disturbed at our arrival.

As we looked down into the crystal-clear water we could see bonito, dolphins, members of the jack family, members of the mackerel family, and many snappers of different kinds— all attracted to our boat by curiosity about this unusual intruder of their privacy. Numerous green turtles came up for a breath of air and a good look at us, but they were careful to keep at a safe distance. Also at a distance we saw several varieties of sharks—a good indication that there were lots of fish nearby, for since sharks feed on fish, they naturally follow the schools.

We could hardly wait to see what great game fish the place would yield. We hoped for some of the rarer kinds—the papagallo, or roosterfish; the pargo, a dog-toothed member of the snapper family; or perhaps the wahoo, a member of the mackerel family. The wahoo plays numerous tricks and is remarkable for its speed when going straight ahead; unfortunately it is fairly uncommon, so that few fishermen know the pleasures of fighting it and subduing its great speed.

Vanderbilt, Jensen, and I took off in a small fishing skiff as soon as it could be lowered over the side. At the southern end of Secas we found an islet separated from the main island by a channel about three hundred yards wide. A current ran through this channel, and this seemed to us to indicate a very good place for game fish.

The islet itself was just a jagged pile of barren rock, the home of thousands of terns which nested there. As we approached in our small boat, they rose in clouds from the rocks and, circling overhead, screeched at us. Maybe they, too, knew their channel was a fine fishing place and were warning us to keep off their preserves.

While we passed through the channel, Vanderbilt and I got ready what we called our prospecting gear: rods, reels, and lines of a medium weight and strength which we used when we were exploring, rather than going after one particular fish. The gear would deal with a tarpon or a marlin, which we were always hoping for, since we had been told to expect them on the Pacific coast of Panama.

When I had finished my preparations, I dropped my bait about one hundred feet out behind the stern. Vanderbilt was intending to do the same, but his line snarled on the reel, and the bait remained on the surface about twenty feet behind. While he was absorbed in trying to right his gear, a great silvery form shot nearly ten feet in the air with the hook firmly in its jaw. Unseen by both of us, it must have leaped at the bait. Because the line was jammed on the reel, the fish broke it at once and escaped, but there was no mistaking it; it was a wahoo.

Before we could do anything more about it, however, I had a bite on my line and was playing a fish none of us could see. It gave us a great fight, but did not jump, so we could not be sure what it was. When I finally managed to bring it near the surface by a manœuvre known as "pumping" (lifting the rod up and down like a pump handle), we found that it was an enormous amberjack, which turned out to weigh eighty pounds. A school of about six others was by its side—evidence of the abundance of fish in these waters—and Vanderbilt soon had one.

We were still thinking of that wahoo, however, and since the boat had by now left the channel, we turned back into it. This time I got a grouper, a member of the same family as the jewfish, but it was seized by a shark. Vanderbilt took a pargo, which gave him a good run before we landed it.

Having left the channel again, we turned back to it a second time. Jensen, who was at the controls, suggested that to attract wahoo we would have to reproduce the conditions under which we hooked the first one so unexpectedly. He cruised through the channel at about ten miles an hour, and we let our baits skid along the surface of the current. We had obviously hit on the right plan, for both Vanderbilt and I hooked a wahoo at the same time.

This made the situation doubly exciting, for each fish decided to go off in different directions. Jensen was compelled to manœuvre between the two fish, allowing one to run at one time and then the other. Frequently the wahoo would change tactics, rushing parallel to the boat instead of away from it, running circles around it, or leaping from the water. But finally we managed to boat them, chiefly because Jensen handled the skiff so well that each of us had plenty of room to play our line without fouling the other's.

No sooner had we caught our first wahoo than we set off after more. It is so rare in an angler's life to have all of these fish he wants, that we took full advantage of our opportunity. Again and again we trolled at high speed through the channel. Although we played many pairs of wahoo, we did not boat very many more; sometimes we lost one or both of them, and sometimes sharks tore them off our hooks. When we returned to the yacht anchored in the bay of our lovely island, we were completely exhausted, but splendidly satisfied.

Later on the same trip we came to a place called Bahia Honda, whose mountains, sweeping down to the water's edge, formed almost a complete circle of protection for the yacht. In some places they were rocky and barren, and in others smothered with tropical vegetation. Brilliant jungle birds and insects and such animals as deer, armadillos, crocodiles, and monkeys lived here.

One August morning Burress, Jensen and I were up before daybreak. We breakfasted by lamplight so as not to lose a minute of the dawn, prepared our tackle, lowered the fishing skiff over the side of the yacht, and waited for the sun to rise. Slowly the light grew stronger in the East, the stars began to disappear, and darkness faded away behind us. The mountains changed from vaguely defined shapes in the blackness to solid bulks with discernible differences in surface. As the sun rose, its rays struck the sea rising and falling beyond our natural harbour; the reflections sparkled with silver.

In this morning splendour we headed out in the skiff to the

open sea. The fish we had caught near the island of Secas had proved even more abundant as we came farther up the coast, and we played quantities of tuna, barracuda, pargo, amberjack and our old friend wahoo. Burress had filmed reel after reel of our battles. Now we wanted to see what this promising water held.

Again we were using the prospecting gear, since we did not know what we might get. As we rode towards a group of islands a few miles out, Burress and I hooked yellowfin tuna, a fish much like the horse-mackerel which had made such havoc of my fishing tackle in New Jersey. Burress lost his to a shark, and mine tore loose, but it was a good beginning.

We hooked on fresh strips of bait and let our lines out again. Peering ahead, Jensen saw a great commotion on the water; he speeded up the boat to reach it. It seemed to be caused by a large fish feeding near the surface, and if it was a large fish, we wanted it.

When we reached the disturbed spot, we began to troll again; as we turned and ran right across it, a bulky fish rose to take my bait with such firmness that we heard the crack of the line tightening against the reel. The reel screeched as the fish turned away in an effort to take more line against the brake. Clenching my teeth, I held on; the fish was terrifically strong and heavy. But Burress took in his line so that it would not foul mine, and we all concentrated on whatever it was I had hooked. With every thrash of his tail the fish seemed to pick up speed; in no time he had taken 200 yards off my shrieking reel.

At the end of this run he suddenly rose half his length out of the water. Then we knew what he was: a roosterfish, or papagallo—a magnificent game fish which is found only in the Pacific. Its four- or five-foot-long body is covered with scales which look like polished silver. On the back are curious greenish-blue markings somewhat like Arabic lettering. The papagallo's dorsal fin bears some resemblance to a sailfish's and is also used for leaping from the water. But the papagallo has even more tricks in its repertoire than the sailfish has; I think it should rank near the top of the list of great game fish.

Our papagallo began a series of jumps and runs which exacted all my strength in efforts to hold the line. Each time it performed its aerial acrobatics, I tried to change its course by throwing it on its side, but it was too strong for me to control in this way. Thrashing furiously on the surface, lunging continually against the strain of the brake and the rod, the papagallo prevented me from retrieving even an inch of my line for more than fifteen minutes.

Now that the fish was securely hooked, I began to worry that my tackle would give way. The leader, which connects the hook to the main line, was made of piano wire, which is not absolutely proof against kinking and breaking; the line itself might break after continual chafing against the fish's rough skin.

When suddenly the line slackened, I knew something of this kind had happened. I began to reel it in, sure that the roosterfish had escaped to freedom—perhaps to fight another angler on another day.

But then I realized that the fish was running *towards* the boat. He might still be hooked; in this case the slack would come from him running towards me, rather than pulling away from me. I reeled furiously, trying to tighten the line before he changed course. As he came within fifty yards of the boat and surfaced again, I was successful; he shook his head in anger in attempts to get rid of the barbed hook in his mouth.

Once again we admired his beauty and his mettle. But he gave us little time for idle appreciation. He shot off again across the bow of the boat, this time remaining near the surface. My line sang out as, for the second time, he took it all.

Again he swung round and again he crossed the bow. At the wheel Jensen had a hard time following his devious tactics, but nothing we did seemed to slow him down. All I could do was to hold on to the line. At every turn he seemed to gather strength, and my reel screamed out repeatedly as he took back the line I had retrieved only a second before.

It is this ability to change course and to summon up new

reserves of energy just when you think it is beaten that makes the papagallo such an exciting fish to play. I was continually amazed as he whipped away from the boat only to double back within twenty yards of it. My arms felt as if they were just about holding in their sockets, and my hands could hardly grip the rod any longer; streams of sweat stung my eyes and ran in rivulets down my neck and back.

My only hope was that the fish would eventually seek safety in the depths of the sea, for at the surface it was easier for him to swim quickly without getting tired. Finally he did sound, but he leaped right up again as if he had just been hooked! I managed, however, to reel in so much line that the leader came up, and Burress was able to lean over the side and sink the gaff hook into his back.

Even then he did not give up. Jensen leaned over too and caught the leader at the swivel where it joins the main line but, determined not to be boated without a real fight, the fish went into a flurry of thrashing and splashing that drenched us all. Jensen and Burress had to boat the fish without me because my arms and shoulders were cramped from holding the rod.

When the papagallo was laid in the bottom of the boat we could do little but stand over it and exclaim, "What a fish!" It was five feet long and its silvery back with the strange markings flashed in the sunlight as it quivered in its death throes. The sight of that fish was like a dream to me, a kind of summit of my angling career.

It was obviously our lucky day, for we caught several more roosterfish during the rest of the afternoon. Sometimes we hooked two at once; then the fun really began! After we had caught more than we could eat, we decided to give the surplus to the inhabitants of a small Indian village which was situated on the shores of Bahia Honda. There proved to be enough roosterfish to feed the entire village, which was extremely happy with our gift. After eating some of the fish right away, the Indians moved out of their huts to cure the rest by smoking them inside.

It is perhaps a pity that roosterfish are not better known as game fish, but, on the other hand, their very rarity makes an encounter with them all the more memorable. I also think it is a great shame that keeping game fish of any kind in an aquarium is a practical impossibility; I should like more people to know and admire them as I do. But because game fish must move rapidly all the time in order to circulate water through their gills, they need more space than an aquarium tank can provide.

Although making a film about game fish was the main purpose of the *White Shadow*'s trip, we did accomplish a certain amount of collecting. Many of the fish we caught were preserved or skinned and sent to taxidermists for eventual inclusion in Vanderbilt's private museum. We did not bring back any fish alive, but we did distribute to various zoos a number of turtles and land animals. These included eleven hawk's bill turtles, seventy baby green turtles, a deer, a white-faced monkey of the type which lives on the island of Coiba, twenty rare birds, a *conejo* (a kind of rabbit), a crocodile, an armadillo, four iguanas, five *gato-solos* (rare cats), and a mangrove cat. We had intended to bring back alive a number of boa constrictors captured in the jungles, but because the crew of the yacht took great exception to their presence aboard, we had to bring them back dead.

On the return journey we again passed through the Panama Canal and stopped to visit the San Blas Indians. For his film Burress wanted as many pictures of these strange people as he could get, so we took great pains to show them that we were very friendly. Surprisingly enough, we found that one of the things they liked best was to see films—which were completely new to them. They never seemed to tire of repeatedly shown newsreels and cartoons; the cartoons were especially fascinating to them.

Our successful film-making venture was greatly assisted by Miss Eleanor Earhart, an American who was living with the Indians at the time. A director of the Columbus, Ohio, School for Deaf Mutes, she was investigating the Indians' educational facilities. She was particularly helpful to Burress in editing and titling his reels.

It must have been a curious existence for a woman among

those people, who inhabit small islands in the Gulf of San Blas and a strip of the northern coast of Panama from San Blas Point to Port Obaldia. Apparently of South American origin, they are a remarkably pure-bred group, for although they have known white men since the sixteenth century, they have successfully resisted foreign settlement on their land. Sometimes they are called White Indians, but this name refers to the unusually high proportion among them of cases of hereditary albinoism.

When we first met them we were immediately impressed by the rings which all the women wear through their noses. When the girls are babies, tiny rings are put through their tender skin, and larger rings are substituted as they grow older.

As we got to know them we saw that they live very primitively. They build houses with palm leaves for roofs, spin and weave in their own homes, squeeze sugar cane by very simple methods, and raise cacao beans, which are sold for export. Also excellent seamen, they can be seen in their dug-out canoes even out of sight of land.

One of the things which interested me most about the San Blas Indians was their way of fishing for tarpon. In the United States the tarpon, a large member of the herring family often called the silver king, is regarded as a great game fish. Although small, rarely exceeding $1\frac{1}{2}$ hundredweight, it can leap high into the air, and it will always give the angler a very good fight. But the San Blas Indians regard the tarpon as a food fish, and not for its flavour but for the quantity of meat to be found on one fish. Distressing as this view is to an angler like me, I must admit that their method of tarpon fishing is in its own way a sport.

Its object is to trap the fish in bays and lagoons and kill them with harpoon-spears. During the winter when tarpon are found in large schools off the coast and islands where the Indians live, they make a funnel-shaped weir across the entrance to a bay by driving in a series of bamboo poles about six inches apart. The "mouth" of the "funnel" opens on the sea, and the "neck", whose entrance is about three feet wide, opens on the bay. To make sure that the fish will swim towards the funnel, the Indians make an additional barrier of poles which extends beyond it into the sea.

When a school is located swimming in the right direction, the men go out in their cayugas, which are made simply by hollowing out a trunk of mahogany, to drive the fish towards the trap. As soon as there are enough fish inside, a bamboo gate is dropped across the opening to prevent them from returning to the open sea.

Then everyone canoes to the inside of the trap and begins to spear tarpon for supper. The harpoon-spear is attached to a man's wrist by a hand-line so that he can throw it and quickly pull it in. He stands poised in his cayuga and aims at a tarpon, hoping to secure it so well that he can pull it back to the boat.

But as often as not he throws himself off balance, capsizes his cayuga, and lands in the water with the frantic fish. Sometimes he spears the fish, but is dragged overboard as the fish tries to wriggle itself free. Or perhaps another cayuga careens into him, and both turn over.

The whole village, from the children to the old people, turns out to line the edge of the bay and watch the sport. Cheering and laughing at the antics of the fishermen, they enjoy the occasion as much as we enjoy a football game. The fun continues into the evening, when the tarpon are finally cooked for a feast. The feast, in turn, usually ends in a performance of strange dances. As is common among primitive peoples, these dances are connected with their religion. The men who dance with prickly leaves hanging down their backs, suffering the pain of the stings as the leaves swing in time to their movements, win special religious merit. For other dances they wear, above their everyday cotton trousers and open shirts, odd hats with wide brims and long leaves sticking straight up out of them.

Our interest in such proceedings and the abundant fish of the Pacific islands made us reluctant to finish our trip. But it was time to go home. We put a box of sand on deck to hatch out some turtle eggs we had used for the film. The very satisfactory results added to the already large collection of animals which were to harass customs officials. With a plan in the back of my mind I asked Vanderbilt if I could have some of these turtles and some of the iguanas. He readily consented, and I had the nucleus of my first collection of live creatures.

7

First Aquarium

IN 1931 after I returned from the expedition with Vanderbilt, I went into partnership with a friend and bought the
Palm Beach Ocean Pier. We set it up as a fishing pier at the
sea end and a tackle shop at the shore end. People paid a small
sum to fish from the pier; on their way on and off they stopped
in the shop to make a purchase or simply to gossip. The
world's record sailfish, which had been skinned and sent back
to the United States for mounting, was displayed in the shop—
the beginning of many a conversation.

All kinds of people came to us. A regular clientele of local
residents, whose characteristics we knew well, appeared every
day, rain or shine. There was one man, for instance, whom
everyone referred to as "Grumpy". Whether the fish were
biting or hiding, he complained. I suppose it was just as well
that he had this outlet for his grudge against life, for otherwise
he would have worked it out on other people.

Among our visitors were men whose names read like a
cross-section of *Who's Who in America*. Members of the
Roosevelt family, the Vanderbilts, and Leon Mandel of the
Mandel Brothers store in Chicago either fished, or bought
their tackle at the pier. My brother Herman, who was now in
the charter boat business in Palm Beach on a full-time basis,
took them on trips around the Florida Keys and the Bahamas.
Because we knew all the best fishing spots, the shop became a
starting and finishing point for many an expedition.

But I wanted people to be interested in fish for their own
sake, not simply as exciting opponents in a game. The plan I
had been mulling over on the *White Shadow* trip, and indeed

long before it, was now to take concrete form. At the inshore end of the pier near the tackle shop, I constructed eighteen small tanks to be filled with sea water and stocked with as complete a collection of Florida fish as I could find. I had one of the state's first aquaria.

Luckily there were few problems in constructing the tanks. They were small—500 gallons each—for at that time no one had thought of bringing large fish, such as sharks and porpoises, into aquaria. The sea water right below the pier had only to be pumped up, and a system by which the water flowed through the tanks was not difficult to work out.

Most of the collection was taken out of the water right off the pier, but some of it I obtained from the reefs which lay just to the east. I took the fish by simply going after them with a net, using the very primitive skin-diving equipment of those days. It consisted merely of goggles over the eyes and a good deep breath, and differed very little from the way in which pearl-divers in the Pacific have carried on their job for centuries. I had been doing this for years, as well as diving in the conventional apparatus of suit and helmet whenever it was available.

By January, 1932, the tanks were all stocked and ready for visitors. Swimming in one of them were the baby turtles I had brought back from the *White Shadow* expedition, and in a room nearby I had fitted up a suitable home for the iguanas.

In the first tank I kept such very small fish as minnows, oysters, sardines, may fish, killifish, dollar fish (which have almost exactly the same shape and size as silver dollars), and hermit crabs. The hermit crabs are especially fascinating creatures, for since they have no shells of their own, they crawl into the empty shells of whelks or other crustacea to make their homes for life. Sea anemones, in turn, often fasten themselves on a hermit's shell for the ride. All these creatures can easily be seen near the Florida shore, but now they could be watched at even closer quarters.

In the second tank I put that silvery-white relation of the pompano which is called a look-down. This fish, I think, is very beautiful, in spite of its permanently turned-down eyes and apparently disdainful expression. When you observe a look-down from the front, because it is so thin it looks like a single vertical line. Schools of look-downs can often be seen hovering in what seems to be an intense study of something directly beneath them. These fish live, by the way, near reefs, but constructions such as sea-walls or the stanchions of a bridge or pier are acceptable substitutes; hence they can easily be caught.

Striped sergeant-majors, which grow to about six inches and are exceedingly prolific, occupied the next tank. Their appearance helps them to blend into the background of the coral reefs where they live.

The fourth tank held the shy razor-fish, creatures of very beautiful colouring which have the curious habit of collecting small bits of coral and broken shell to make themselves houses. Once the houses are built, they rarely move far from them. The razor-fish in the tank went about their building just as they would have done in the sea, for we had provided coral and shells for them.

With them lived some more very bright reef fish, including members of the snapper and grunt family. (Grunts, by the way, get their name because that is exactly what they do when they are taken out of the water.) In the same tank were some yellow-tailed damselfish, lovely-looking creatures with purple bodies and yellow tails, but with rather unpleasant dispositions They will fight any other little fish put in with them and pick at them until their lives are not worth living.

The fifth tank contained our green turtles and some hawk's bill turtles, the ones whose shells are used for so-called tortoise-shell products. There were not as many turtles as we had had when we left Panama, for when we reached Havana, we were so delayed by Customs officials, who were deciding whether or not to let the turtles enter Cuba, that many of them died waiting.

The next few tanks held groupers, the slow-moving relations of the jewfish; porgies, which are well known as food fish; and some more snappers. Snappers, incidentally, are so called because they have very sharp teeth and will bite anything which threatens them; if you pick one up, it will very likely seize a part of your hand and be most reluctant to let go.

In the ninth tank I kept pufferfish, amberjack, and specimens of a game fish known as the jack cravalla. Pufferfish are small and greenish-yellow with scales rather like small prickles. When you take a pufferfish out of the water, or otherwise frighten it, it inflates rapidly so that its bluish-white underbelly becomes taut. It deflates again when put back in the water. This mechanism is one of nature's devices for preserving life, for when an enemy comes along to eat the puffer, it simply swells up so much that the enemy can't get it into its mouth.

Some toadfish, which are extremely ugly creatures, also lived in this tank. Greyish-brown to match the bottom of the sea, where they spend their lives, they are covered with soft spines, which bristle when they are aroused. Toadfish are one of the few types of fish which nest in the old cans, boots, and other debris that man has supplied so liberally to the sea.

The tenth tank held whiting, thread fins, croakers, and other fish which are often seen on the edge of surf and could be caught in hundreds from our pier.

Next door I had several kinds of triggerfish, who protect themselves against enemies by an unusual mechanical arrangement. When a triggerfish is in danger, the three spines on its back become erect and so rigid that it is impossible to push them down into the body. They will break off sooner than fold. But if a certain one of the spines—the "trigger"—is merely pressed lightly, all three will retract.

In another tank were some more grunts, most of whom had the brilliant red mouth characteristic of their species. Nearby was a glamorous French angelfish, whose eyes and black scales were rimmed with gold. Gay yellow, blue, and white butterfly fish, which flutter round their native reefs like a butterfly round flowers, looked less sophisticated than the angelfish but just as attractive. Also exhibited were some relations of the butterfly fish, called four-eyed butterflies because of a large black spot just in front of the tail on each side. These markings look like another pair of eyes.

Not far away was a species of snapper (different from the kind I kept near the porgies and jewfish) and a moonfish. A moonfish somewhat resembles a look-down, but its forehead does not slope in the same way, and its dorsal and ventral fins do not have the look-down's elongated points.

The seventeenth tank housed a filefish, whose rough skin can be used as sandpaper and which used to be nailed up in fishing boats for striking matches; a surgeon fish, who uses the sharp lancet-like spine near its tail to attack enemies; and some brilliantly coloured parrotfish, whose mouths look exactly like parrots' beaks. When they swim, these fish seem to be "rowing", because of the peculiar action of their pectoral fins (the pair of fins nearest to the head). Since they graze naturally on vegetation, parrotfish help to keep the tanks in which they live free from algae and other plants.

In separate quarters I kept an exhibit of octopuses—not for their beauty, for certainly they have none, but for their ability to inspire terror. I have learned that it thrills people to be frightened by such creatures at a close, but safe, distance.

With the same psychology in mind I filled a nearby tank with moray eels, long and slimy things which have been called the rattlesnakes of the ocean. Although they look green when they are swimming, if you take them out of the water you find that they are really blue; the yellow slime covering them gives them a green tinge. A bite from the wicked little teeth in their pointed mouths would certainly be toxic.

Another poisonous creature, the scorpion fish, shared this watery chamber of horrors. The scorpion fish stays for long periods on the bottom of the sea, where, despite its untidy-looking spines and fins, it is hard to spot. Mottled and blotched on a background of colour much like a rock, it is a hazard to the unwary bather. If he places a foot on it, it leaves a very nasty—and sometimes fatal—sting.

None of these fish were in any way rare, but the existence of the collection was for me a great step forward. At last I had a place in which to keep fish alive. The responsibilities of collecting, owning, and keeping them taught me a great deal that was to make later jobs of the same sort easier to handle.

The aquarium prospered: it was received enthusiastically by the people who came to use the pier, and I was continually getting more specimens. The collection was described at great length in a Florida newspaper, and before long tourists who were not fishermen were coming to the pier to see it.

Although I certainly would not have been able to accommodate one, I very nearly got a whale for my first aquarium. As my brother Herman was fishing one day a long way out from Palm Beach, he came upon a huge finback, which he decided to harpoon and bring into Palm Beach. But he didn't realize what a job that would be with only a forty-foot cruiser and two men.

Throughout a day and a half, the two men held on to the whale, unable to kill it but unwilling to let it go. Other fishermen in the vicinity saw what was going on and returned to Palm Beach to tell me that my brother had a sixty-foot finback. They urged me to bring him a gun and several rounds of ammunition. With several other people from Palm Beach I raced to his aid in a boat called *Let's Go*, which I owned at the time.

The whale did not die until three or four hundred rounds of ammunition had been used on it. Then we were presented with the problem of bringing it in; we finally had to send for a tug to tow it into the Palm Beach Inlet.

As long as the whale remained fresh, it was a strong attraction for visitors and residents. But soon we had to dispose of it. We had to tow most of the flesh far out to sea, but I kept the huge jaw bones and made them into an arch for the entrance to the pier. As far as I know, they are still there.

In spite of the aquarium, the tackle shop, and the many visitors to the pier, I had plenty of time for fishing expeditions of my own, either alone or with friends. It was on one of these expeditions, in company with two other anglers, that I saw the largest fish in the world.

The creature which holds this distinction is the whale shark, or *Rhineodon typus*, as it is officially titled. It can reach a length of more than forty feet and a weight of ten to fifteen tons. Because it has a vertical tail and breathes through its gills, it is classified as a fish, but like the whale, which is of course a mammal, it bears its young alive and one at a time. Both whale and whale shark feed on plankton—minute animals sometimes so small that they cannot be seen without a microscope. The whale shark filters plankton from the water by straining it through its fine gill-rakers, as do most whales. Its mouth cavity is large enough to hold a man, but its throat is too small to swallow even an object the size of a grapefruit. The teeth are very small, but there are very many of them, so that the jaws are covered with a formation rather like a coarse grade of sandpaper. On a whale shark twenty-three feet long the teeth were found to be two millimetres, or .079 inches long. Certainly neither the whale nor the whale shark would have been able to swallow Jonah!

Whale sharks are solitary creatures which can be found in all the temperate oceans of the world. Since they do not frequent any particular part of the ocean, they can be found quite unexpectedly almost anywhere, except in shallow water near the shoreline. Here they seldom venture. They have no defences against their enemies except their immensity and the toughness of their hides, which some harpooners and riflemen nevertheless try to pierce. Such "sport" is not very rewarding, for the whale shark is a sitting target which doesn't give the fisherman much chance to show skill; it is of no value, moreover, when dead.

The day we discovered the whale shark three of us were cruising along the north-east fringes of the Bahamas in search of game fish or interesting exhibits for the aquarium. We were about five miles east of Walker's Key, where the ocean was glassy calm, when one of my friends, who was acting as a kind of look-out, saw a mysterious object two miles away. He suggested that we go towards the spot, where there seemed to be some commotion on the surface.

As I brought the boat in quietly and with caution, we saw before us a huge spotted form gliding beneath the waves. We passed it, noting that it was nearly as long as our forty-six-foot cruiser and nearly as large in girth as our boat was wide. The creature's back was bluish-black with white blotches that (*right*) Close-up of the mola-mola. It weighs about four hundredweight and is about six feet long.

(*below*) Another view of the rare mola-mola.

(*Photo: courtesy the Seaquarium*)

(*above*)   The birth of a porpoise, tail first.

(*below*)   Just born at the Seaquarium after the normal eleven-month gestation period, this porpoise will be weaned from its mother after about eighteen months.

(*Photo: courtesy UPI*)

A tiger shark being walked by a diver at Marine Studios.

(*above*) A shark in the Seaquarium channel slaps at its meal of fish suspended from the bridge above.

(*below*) The lemon shark at dinner.

(*Photos: courtesy the Seaquarium*

(*Photo: courtesy UPI*)

(*above*)   The diver vacuuming the floor of the Seaquarium tank pays little attention to the tiger shark.

(*below*)   Here I am injecting vitamin B-12 into a pilot whale as a stimulant to help it adjust to captivity.

Jim Kline, porpoise trainer at the Seaquarium, treats one of his charges
for a sore eye.

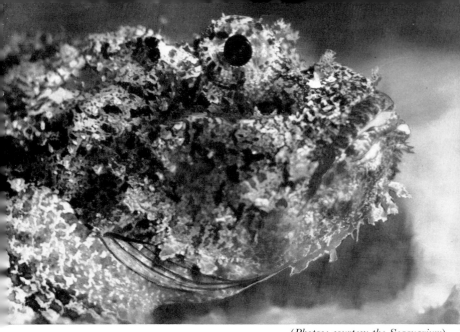

(*Photos: courtesy the Seaquarium*)

(*above*) The soft protuberances of the rare scorpionfish conceal poison-bearing spines.

(*below*) If you were to step on this toadfish in the ocean it would grab a toe and hold on.

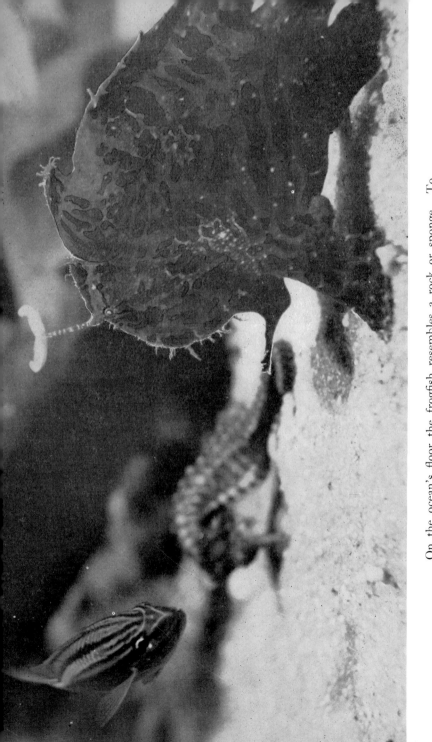

On the ocean's floor the frogfish resembles a rock or sponge. To attract prey it ejects an antenna with a worm-like lure.

were arranged in a draughtsboard pattern—a design that looked especially impressive with the ocean's blue superimposed on it. Behind the irregularly rounded head were two pectoral fins, rather like arms.

As I turned the boat and moved as close to the fish as I could, so that we could follow it and observe its habits, it showed no signs of panic. It seemed quite content to swim along slowly and continue its feeding. Several times we were near enough to it to jump from the boat to its back.

We realized we could not take in this fish alive, but since we did not want to kill it, we just kept pace with it for a few hours to take pictures of it with still and motion picture cameras and to study it. Although I had to look after the wheel, I also took pictures when I had a chance, and one of these was unusually successful. As the fish passed under the boat, about six feet below the surface, I just happened to click the camera. The result showed the pattern of the fish's skin very clearly. I was so proud of it that I have an enlargement hanging on my office wall even now.

We noticed that the whale shark fed on plankton by skimming the water with its great mouth open, its head half out, its dorsal fin mostly out, and its tail cutting the surface. Its favourite feeding place, we noticed, was along what is called a tide-rip, where two different currents in the ocean come together. You can easily see a tide-rip because it is usually marked by a collection of floating seaweed and flotsam (floating objects cast off or swept off from a boat). Drifting with one current and rejected by the other, the seaweed and flotsam are endlessly tossed between them. At such a junction plankton abounds.

Although this was a day without the thrill of battling a game fish or landing something of record size, I still remember it for one of my greatest fishing successes. What I brought home was not something I could hang up on the pier, but an experience shared by all too few. If I ever manage to capture a small whale shark (it is not possible to bring home a large one), many more people will better understand the meaning of my adventure.

6

But to realize fully the awesome quality of the whale shark it is necessary to see one fully grown. It is the size of whales, I think, which is so fascinating to men. Moby Dick's massiveness, as well as his whiteness, amazed the crew of the *Pequod*.

Perhaps whales themselves don't always know how to handle their bulk. At any rate a story told to me by a friend of mine suggests this.

It was off Brown's Bank, eighty miles out from Nova Scotia, on a June night in the early 1930s that the incident he related occurred. A schooner, captained by my friend Henry LeBlanc, had hove to for the night; LeBlanc and six members of his crew were enjoying a good sleep below, while one man on deck stood the watch.

Suddenly the schooner was struck from below by a shock which tossed all the men from their bunks to the floor.

In the confusion that resulted, they thought that somehow the schooner had been rammed. When they all scrambled up on deck, however, they saw a huge whale thrashing furiously about in the water near the boat. After shaking its head and turning round, it disappeared beneath the surface and was seen no more.

Apparently it had risen to the surface to breathe—as whales must do—directly under the schooner. It was that impact which caused the great shock. The whale then lifted the vessel almost entirely out of the water before it plunged over on its side and fell back into the sea. This caused the schooner to rock so violently that the man on deck watch nearly fell overboard.

I imagine that the poor creature, which only wanted a breath of air, was just as amazed as the men by what its bulk had done.

Luckily the whale had not damaged the propeller, so the crew started up the engine as quickly as possible and headed into Yarmouth. There the boat was put into dry dock. No damage to the bottom of the boat was found, which is not surprising because the back of a whale is soft and flexible. If it had bumped against the rudder, shaft, and propeller, however, it might well have broken one or all three.

8

Tuna Again

BONEFISH are often described as the gamest of all sports fish, in spite of their relatively small size. Although they never run heavier than sixteen pounds, they will fight like a fish weighing three times that much.

I have been bonefishing for many years and find it so fascinating that I doubt if I will ever have my fill. The fish are extremely intelligent and temperamental; it requires great patience to make them take the hook and great endurance to play them, for they have many tricks to outwit the angler. But once they have been brought to the boat, it is usual to release them again, for they are rarely eaten by anyone except the natives of the Bahama Islands.

Their unpredictability is one of their greatest attractions. I have spent hours stalking them, in large or small schools, singly or in pairs, over shallow flats, in deep channels, at low tide, high tide, or in between—using crawfish, shrimp, hermit crabs and conch for bait—and not taken a single fish. Yet on one day in June, 1934, four of us in a party caught and released 114 bonefish—a tremendous achievement, for five or six in a day should be enough to keep anybody happy.

Long before my friend and I owned the Palm Beach Pier I had been chasing bonefish, but it was during this time that I caught my biggest one. It was no world record, but to me it was a source of great satisfaction.

The adventure started when I went with some friends to fish off the native settlement at West End in the Grand Bahamas. When we had anchored the boat and landed I met an old friend of mine, a Negro called Teddy Grant. Teddy was well known as the best bonefishing guide in the island; he had the sport in his blood. He fished with a hand-line, which for going after game fish is quite a feat, and he made a good living selling the bonefish he caught to the natives, who considered it a great delicacy.

He told me when I stopped to talk with him that he had seen a school of extra-large bonefish at Sandy Bay. He suggested that the fishing would be best at high tide, when we could catch the fish as they ran into the bay from the open sea.

The two of us collected a great deal of crawfish and conch for bait and rowed off just before sundown in a small skiff. Teddy picked a spot just inside the entrance of Sandy Bay where there were no coral snags (miniature reefs along the bottom) and where the water was about three feet deep. He put stakes into the sand bottom at each end of the boat and tied it securely to them so that the boat would not swing. We wished to avoid every possible noise or disturbance which might frighten our very nervous bonefish.

Teddy cut up the bait into small pieces and scattered it away from the boat in the same way as we would chum for tuna if we were cruising. I used light tackle without a sinker, which would have made a loud *plunk* as it hit the water; at such shallow spots a chunk of bait about the size of a walnut gives sufficient weight to cast.

Teddy got his hand-line ready, and the two of us sat patiently in the growing darkness. We made as little movement as possible; a great stillness and silence seemed to cover the whole world. Every now and then our lines would be taken by a small snapper, and the jerk would startle us. We boated a few of these and waited.

As soon as the tide started running in—the "young flood" as Teddy called it—he hooked a bonefish. Manipulating his hand-line without a single snarl, he played the fish for a while and then landed it, a beautiful seven-pounder.

We threw out some more chum. Suddenly I was startled by a hard pull on my line; I set the hook in what I was sure was a huge bonefish. I played it for several minutes and it gave me a furious fight, but when I boated it, it turned out to be a five-pound snapper—a tough fighter in its own way and something to be proud of at any time except when you're out for bonefish.

During most of the next hour we sat and waited, although Teddy did catch another bonefish of about five pounds, and I lost one after playing it for a few minutes.

Then I felt a slight tug on my line which I thought was a small fish of some sort trying to steal my bait. I gave the rod a quick jerk and to my surprise I felt the hook set solidly. Before I knew what had happened, whatever I had caught had stripped two-thirds of my line from the reel and was still running away.

"That's him!" exclaimed Teddy in great excitement as he cut the ropes which bound the boat to the stakes and scrambled in the pitch darkness for the oars. About one hundred and fifty yards of my line were out by the time Teddy managed to get the boat under way.

He pulled frantically on the oars to try to keep up with the fish as it fled into the bay. It made a zigzag course, occasionally lit up with flashes of phosphorescence in the darkness, over very hazardous water: numerous jagged coral snags on the bottom could have very easily broken my line at the slightest contact.

As Teddy rowed hard, I managed to play the fish, but although I gained line once or twice, I soon lost it again. In a quarter of an hour we had travelled so far up the bay that we were opposite the dim lights of the settlement houses. Now Teddy slowed down a little and told me that we were clear of the coral snags and above the shallow flats in about three feet of water. I thought the rest of the game would be relatively easy. I felt that I had the fish fairly well under control and was carefully avoiding the temptation to force him near the boat or to hold him too hard when he lunged away.

When I had worked him to about twenty feet away from the boat, the fish made a quick run round the stern. I stepped up on the stern sheets, holding the rod high and out as far as I could reach to allow the line to follow him. I was slightly off balance in this position and when I stepped on a piece of conch we had left on the sheets to use as bait, overboard I went in the least graceful of falls.

Since the bonefish is a sensitive fish, we had been taking every precaution not to frighten him. But when I practically fell on top of him—and I am not small—the fish was seized with panic.

Before I could recover my balance to stand in the shallow water my line was all out. I managed to prevent it from breaking by following the fish—walking when I could and swimming when I had to by paddling with one hand as I held the line with the other. Teddy, who was doubtless disgusted with me for frightening my catch so clumsily, kept up with me in the boat, but I could not attempt to get back in it until I had retrieved some line.

At last the fish changed his panicky course, enabling me to take in about fifty yards and scramble into the boat. By this time he was exhausted. I brought him gently alongside the boat; Teddy slipped his fingers under the gills and lifted him over the side.

It is a tribute to the bonefish as a fighter that this one which weighed only ten and one half pounds had given us such a struggle. I was very proud to show it to my companions on the trip, but not quite so proud to tell them how I nearly frightened it to death.

The bonefish's relative, the tarpon, has also given me a great deal of sport, and on one occasion, a great disappointment. I once helped catch, and witnessed the loss of, a tarpon bigger than I had imagined in my wildest dreams.

A good friend and I had taken a small fishing skiff with oars and an outboard motor for a week's tarpon fishing at Bahia Honda, below Marathon in the Florida Keys. This was in early May, when the tarpon were coming in great numbers through a cut between two keys; it appears that they stayed there for a time before moving into Florida Bay, between the Keys and the mainland, and then upwards into the Gulf of Mexico on the west coast of Florida. The angler who fished in the cut, which was very deep, could be fairly certain at least to hook a fish, if not land one.

It was late in the afternoon when we got the skiff launched; on our very first trip through the cut we each hooked a tarpon, but lost it almost immediately. Several times we ran through the cut back and forth, taking several fish, losing some of them and in one or two fights losing a little tackle.

Then my friend suddenly hooked a fish which did not leap out of the water immediately as a tarpon usually does. It went down very deep for several minutes, while we wondered what it could possibly be. Then at last it burst out of the water, and we saw a tarpon of such size that it was almost frightening. It looked almost as long as our skiff, and I felt sure it would weigh nearly two hundredweight.

Neither of us could say a word. My friend began to play the fish, and I reeled in my line to avoid fouling his. I took up the oars, ready for battle.

At the end of two hours the tarpon seemed as strong as ever. In spite of all I could do with the oars, we were two miles out on the seaward side of Bahia Honda and before long we would be in the Gulf Stream. The sun was going down fast. The situation began to look critical, for if we were to get in the Gulf Stream in the dark, we would probably be forced to give up the tarpon in order to save ourselves.

I used to row a boat when I was younger as part of my fisherman's trade, but I doubt if I ever rowed harder in my life than I did in the next hour while we tried to persuade our tarpon to come back to the Bahia Honda cut. Our efforts did tell a little, for if we were not exactly gaining, neither were we heading into the Atlantic. It looked as if we had a chance of bringing the tarpon in, so I strained at the oars and my friend played him just a little harder.

Then we saw a high dorsal fin, the sign of a shark, appear on the surface behind him. There was a short flurry in the water; the open mouth of a hammerhead shark engulfed most of the tarpon, closed, and sank.

There was nothing we could do. Silently my friend reeled in his line. We decided to go ashore as fast as we could, for the disappointment had taken the heart out of us. I pulled and pulled for all I was worth at the starter of the outboard motor, but nothing happened. Although I was very tired after our fight with the tarpon, I had no choice but to row in.

Since the tide was ebbing and I did not have the strength to make headway against it, we threw out the anchor with the intention of waiting for the tide to come in again before we set out. There was no equipment to speak of aboard our tiny boat. To indicate where we were I had to improvise a beacon light. I dipped my handkerchief in the petrol tank, tied it to the tip of my fishing rod, and lit it with a match.

Shortly afterwards we were relieved to hear the sound of an outboard motor. Two fishermen friends of ours who had seen us set out in the afternoon and had not seen us return had come to look for us. We told them our sad tale and thankfully accepted the offer of a tow.

The friend who shared my disappointment told me that he and his wife, a fishing enthusiast with as much skill as he, had previously had a tough time at Marathon, just north of where we had encountered the tarpon. He and his wife disagree on the details of their encounter with a barracuda, but apart from that they are an extremely compatible pair.

Now a barracuda is a vicious creature which grows as long as six feet and has a long, slim build rather like a pike's. In its very wide mouth is a set of knife-sharp teeth, which are capable of terrible damage. Many of the attacks on bathers which are attributed to sharks are, in fact, the work of the barracuda. It will follow any moving object and is especially dangerous in cloudy water, where it easily becomes panicky.

My friend's tale began after he and his wife had fished all morning for bonefish. With great enjoyment each had taken and released two bonefish; no cause for squabbles here! When the tide turned and the bonefish disappeared, they decided to catch some spiny lobsters for a good evening meal. They pulled up the stakes which held their boat, just as Teddy's had held ours off Sandy Bay, and cruised gaily to a reef where the water was waist-deep. Wearing cotton gloves to pick up the lobsters and carrying glass-bottomed buckets, they waded after their dinner. They did not stick the lobsters with spears, as so many people do, but grabbed them alive and stowed them in the bottom of the boat. It is kind to kill lobsters by boiling rather than spearing them, and it also makes a superior meal.

The couple also brought up a few conch shells, from which they would extract the pink conch for a seafood salad. They filled the bottom of the boat with the shells and the spiny lobsters, started the motor, and relaxed for the homeward trip. My friend took off his shoes, an act which later proved his undoing, and rested his feet on the gunwales, while his wife sat amidships. Since they were about a mile from shore, my friend began trolling, just to see what was there.

Apparently nothing was there, until he began to reel in his line as they neared their dock. Suddenly the line drew so taut that he was nearly thrown out of the boat. He cut down the motor without stopping it and jumped, barefooted, to the stern sheets; he couldn't stand on the bottom of the boat because of the lobsters.

Before he knew what he had on the line, it burst out of the water right beside the boat and landed smack in it. Both husband and wife saw at once that it was a barracuda, and a big one. Spiny lobsters, conch shells, bait, and tackle flew in all directions as the barracuda thrashed about in the boat.

At this point the couple begin to disagree; my friend says he fell overboard and his wife says he jumped. In any case, he found himself in the water, and the poor woman was left in the boat with a fifty-pound very-much-alive barracuda. She took an oar and tried to hit it on the head, but every time she managed to bring the oar down, the fish wriggled away.

Meanwhile the boat was still moving out with the motor in low gear, and my friend was swimming alongside it, hoping there were no more barracudas in the vicinity. At last his wife, still laying about her with the oar, managed to get into the stern and away from the barracuda long enough to speed up the motor. Directing her husband to grab on to the side of the skiff, she towed him to shallow water, where he was able to get in the boat and help her kill the barracuda.

They are probably still arguing about whether he jumped or fell.

While this and other adventures were taking place in the

early thirties, stories kept reaching us from Bimini in the Bahamas of fish so big that they snapped everything they were hooked with. I remembered my similar experience with the horse-mackerel in 1909 and I felt sure that these big fish were the same ones—bluefin tuna, to give them their correct name.

But since for a long time none of the big Bimini fish were brought to gaff, I had no way of verifying my hunch. The natives and the many visitors who were attracted by hopes of catching the fish gave such widely varying descriptions that it was hard to guess what they had actually seen. It sounded as if some of them had even seen very large members of the shark family.

Finally in early 1934 the owner of a fishing club on Cat Key, near Bimini, succeeded in landing one of the monsters. This turned out to be a marlin—a close relative of the sword-fish—weighing $4\frac{1}{2}$ hundredweight and measuring twelve feet. It was brought to Miami, where a large crowd collected to see it. When it was realized that fish of this size and beauty were to be taken, there was a rush of enthusiasts to Bimini.

A number of Florida fishing guides, men who earned their livings taking out fishing parties on a charter basis, collected their heaviest gear and left for Bimini in a race to land another of the huge fish. As soon as I could get away from my responsibilities at the Palm Beach Pier, I joined them. On June 1st, 1934, I crossed to Bimini with three friends.

When we arrived the place was full of excitement, for two brothers, both charter boat captains from Miami, had just brought in the head of a tuna. The other part of the fish had been seized by sharks, just as our tarpon had. But since the head weighed 3 hundredweight and was fifty-seven inches round, the rest could be imagined. The stories we heard from other fishermen indicated that this fish was the one which was breaking everyone's tackle. My hunch had proved right: once again I was going to fight tuna.

But except for assuring us it was tuna we were after, the reports were not very helpful.

"The fish was as big round as a barrel!" one man exclaimed.

"It smashed my rod before I knew what had happened," said another.

"After hours of fighting I nearly had him gaffed, and then the leader broke," a third fisherman mourned.

"It snapped my fifty-four thread like string," said another, completely baffled.

"That fish was stone dead, 200 yards down straight, and I couldn't lift him an inch," was still another tale.

The tackle the fishermen had desperately lined up was as varied as their stories. The brothers who had brought in the tuna were using huge all-metal reels they had designed especially for such big fish. These reels held a thousand yards of the heaviest line I had ever seen. To prevent the line from searing their forearms in the struggle the brothers had also provided themselves with leather wristlets which reached up to their elbows. Obviously it was this equipment which allowed them to be as successful as they were.

Other anglers had very heavy sports fishing tackle. One reinforced his line with half a mile of sash cord, neatly coiled in a washtub on deck. Another had a drum filled with quarter-inch bronze cable attached to a winch. The winch was bolted to the deck of the cockpit and was turned with power supplied by the boat's motor.

My three friends and I looked at our ordinary sports fishing tackle with very little confidence. But we decided to give it a try.

Soon after we started out the next morning, with our lines fixed to outriggers so they wouldn't foul on one another, I hooked something large which I thought was a tuna. But when we boated it, it proved to be a forty-pound kingfish, a prize at any other time, but now only useful as strip bait.

Shortly afterwards we saw and felt what seemed like a depth charge behind the boat. At once we gripped our rods; the reels screeched as the lines whirled off. A second later we were reeling them in—broken. We never saw what had caused the havoc.

During our stay in Bimini we came no closer to boating a tuna. Sometimes we managed to hang on to one for about an hour, sometimes for half that time. Then the line would break or the rod snap, and nothing more could be done. On one occasion my reel spun so quickly that it got hot and jammed, causing the rod to break and the line to part.

One of our party boated a white marlin which weighed seventy-five pounds, but apart from that we took back only a large quantity of broken tackle. As in 1909, I had lost my fight with the tuna.

Later in 1934 Ernest Hemingway was the first man to bring in a tuna whole. He caught it, hung on to it for two hours and fifty minutes, and eventually brought it in to Bimini, where it tipped the scales at $2\frac{3}{4}$ hundredweight.

After this, great progress was made in the design of tackle and during the next season at Bimini, in the early summer of 1935, there was a much greater degree of success. It is often said that most of angling is "preparations and expectations". And it was obvious that many of the anglers who again flooded Bimini for the season had spent the intervening time preparing their tackle. They brought newly-designed reels, triple-strength rods, and leaders made of aircraft wire instead of the usual piano wire. Some of this equipment had been tested by towing boats and even automobiles.

Not all of this tackle, however, stood the test of the tuna, and it was only in the hands of competent anglers that even the best of it did any good. It was still a great accomplishment —a matter of physical strength as well as skill—to land a huge tuna all in one piece.

Michael Lerner, a member of the family which owns Lerner Shops, was one of the earliest and most capable tuna fishing enthusiasts. In 1935 he was so successful at Bimini that when the season ended he decided to follow the fish as they proceeded north. He became a pioneer of tuna fishing off Nova Scotia.

During their lives tuna are known to migrate from the South Atlantic to the North Atlantic and back again. We knew that they stayed around Bimini until late in June, and as a result of later experience we learned that from July 4th to Labour Day they could be caught in great abundance off Nova Scotia.

From there they seem to go even farther north before turning south at the beginning of the winter to begin the circle once more.

When Lerner went to Nova Scotia in 1935, however, in company with Bimini's best tuna guide, he did not know exactly where he would find what he was looking for. All he knew was that since the time of the earliest settlers tuna had been seen off Nova Scotia, where they were considered a nuisance because, just as off the New Jersey coast, they caused havoc to commercial fishing.

Lerner and the guide explored many miles of water along the south side of Nova Scotia, but found no tuna. Everywhere they heard the same story: "If you had only been here last month, you'd have had all the tuna you wanted and more." Becoming increasingly discouraged, they finally packed up and went to Yarmouth to take the steamer home.

In Yarmouth, however, they heard a different tale. Everyone told them that although no tuna were there, plenty were to be had at Wedgeport only seventeen miles away. This story was too convincing to be ignored; Lerner and the guide went to Wedgeport.

There they talked with local fishermen, who promised to take them out the next morning on their lobster boats. When they kept their promise, Lerner, who had taken along his special heavy tackle, soon hooked a tuna and brought it to the boat. The local men were astonished because it was the first time in this part of Nova Scotia that a tuna had been taken with rod and reel. As soon as the news got out, fishermen began to take a great interest in Nova Scotia.

After Lerner's first catch his companion spent the rest of the day rigging up a makeshift fishing chair, foot braces and shoulder harness; he wanted to be ready for an early start next day in a hired boat. The tuna were running all along the tide-rips which are typical of this coast, and in the next seven days Lerner took twenty-one bluefins.

Before he was finished several other anglers had arrived from the States to take advantage of the run. But it was now September, and the season was nearly over. Only a few more tuna were boated before the fishermen went home to plan an early return the following year.

From a fisherman's point of view the discovery of abundant tuna at Wedgeport was comparable to the discovery of gold in Alaska. The businessmen of Wedgeport and the surrounding districts were also delighted, for they realized that with them the fishermen would bring a great deal of trade. In 1936 the mayor and the city fathers prepared Wedgeport for the expected influx of visitors. Under their guidance the Wedgeport Tuna Guides' Association was organized to give visitors the best fishing available. Twenty-five boats with their captains and crews were enrolled in the Association during the early part of 1936.

To help the Association members convert their lobster boats into suitable tuna-fishing vessels and to teach them all the tricks of tuna sports fishing, it was felt that a director was needed. Since I was well known as a sports fisherman and since I had been one of the first to fight tuna off Bimini and, very much earlier, off New Jersey, I was appointed Director of the Tuna Guides' Association. In the spring of 1936 I gave up my interest in the Palm Beach Pier and deserted my first aquarium. I was determined to get even with the tuna, my old enemies.

9

Tales from Wedgeport

D URING the next five years, from 1936 to 1941, I spent the summers at Wedgeport directing tuna fishing operations. For the rest of each year I was free to go anywhere I chose on collecting expeditions and sports fishing trips.

Our operations at Wedgeport were so outstandingly successful that Wedgeport became internationally known as a centre for sports tuna fishing. During the very first season in 1936 President Roosevelt, then nearing the end of his first term, spent a day fishing here. I accompanied the President, who did not get a tuna, but afterwards sent a letter saying how much he had enjoyed his excursion.

Wedgeport became famous as a place where monster tuna were to be taken. Nearly every year a local or national record was established, only to be broken the following year. In 1939 John Manning, who later turned from sports fishing to oceanography, landed a world's record tuna which weighed 8 hundredweight. A year later Mrs. Lyman C. Bloomingdale of New York brought in a tuna which weighed 7 hundredweight and became the world's record catch for a woman.

As director of fishing operations, I had to show my paces each season; I usually managed to land the first tuna about July 4 or July 6. It was rarely above 4½ hundredweight, but that is quite respectable as a send-off.

Tackle had, of course, been improved by the time Wedgeport became a tuna-fishing centre. Heavy equipment was now standard. But a catch still depended—as it always will—on the skill and endurance of the angler.

We tried all kinds of things to attract the fish, and in 1938 we perfected a system of chumming with a number of herring. In an article I wrote about this system for *Hunting and Fishing* I described how odd our boats looked with a string of small fish trailing from the stern and how successful these fish were as bait. Our gimmick was based upon experience with the huge schools of tuna at the tide-rips. We were able to obtain comparatively few strikes with the use of a single line and bait, but we noticed that the tuna would repeatedly strike into schools of herring. We decided to see if we could reproduce a school of herring—but with hooks inside.

At first the only way we could think to do this was to tie herring-baited leaders at frequent intervals to a broomstick. We trolled with the broomstick floating out behind. People laughed at this queer contraption, but they respected the results. Since the tuna were suspicious at first, we threw out some whole herring as chum, and soon the tuna were biting the herring with hooks in them.

Luckily it was discovered soon afterwards that a few herring strung to a line could replace the exceedingly clumsy broomstick arrangement. From then on we had no trouble at all; tremendous numbers of tuna were hooked all summer.

Along the tide-rips we found that a boat running its motor at a fast trolling speed would just hold its own against the current. Thus we could troll all day there, where the tuna were thickest, without actually going anywhere. This is where we took the anglers, who as often as not brought in more fish to add to our summer's total; in 1940 the total weight of tuna taken at Wedgeport was $18\frac{3}{4}$ tons.

To add to the fun, the officials of Wedgeport decided to organize an international tuna-fishing tournament. Since most of the visiting anglers were American or Canadian, there was a ready-made contest of nationalities. In addition, we had anglers from Cuba, and we hoped later on to attract Europeans.

In 1937 the first tournament took place, between opposing seven-man teams representing the United States and the British Empire. For some reason I was chosen coach of the British Empire team; I was unpatriotically delighted to see my team win the trophy by nine points to three. Unfortunately during the second year of the tournament there was such bad weather that the fourteen contestants caught only five tuna.

In 1938 the tournament was scheduled at Liverpool, Nova Scotia; a Cuban team won. By 1939 there were entries from France and Belgium, plus the original Western Hemisphere countries. It looked as if the event scheduled for early September would be a tough contest, but the outbreak of the war scotched our plans. The teams dispersed to their countries, and for eight or nine years there was no talk of international sport at Wedgeport.

Before the war ended our activities here, our enjoyment in action had been enriched by the fun of swapping "fish stories". One of our favourites was about a man and his two sons who were cruising off the Nova Scotia coast in a motor boat when they harpooned a tuna. Now to play a harpooned tuna, you have to chase it from a smaller boat to which the harpoon line is usually attached and which is launched from a larger boat after the harpoon has been struck. The tale goes that after the man had harpooned his tuna and leaped into the small boat, the tuna took control like a horse running away with the bit. He towed the fisherman in the small boat so fast that the motor boat could not keep up. Before long the man had disappeared into the fog which often shrouds this coast.

During the day his two sons made strenuous but unsuccessful efforts to find him; when night came on, the darkness and fog were a double hindrance. The next morning several boats joined the search, but no trace of the boat could be found.

Until noon of that day everyone feared the worst.

But then the missing man telephoned from a harbour about ten miles away to say that he was enjoying a hearty breakfast.

When he returned, he told his sons that the tuna had towed him for many miles without stopping and that it had changed course so many times he had no idea where he was. Suddenly the fish was stopped by something in front; the man was stranded, apparently nowhere, in the middle of the night in a cold fog. To prevent getting numb all over he had to jump around, or otherwise keep moving, all night.

In the morning some fishermen who came out from the harbour were surprised to find in their herring nets not only a good catch but a 7-hundredweight tuna attached to a boat, and a very cold man! Apparently the tuna had headed straight for the nets, tangled itself up so that it could not move, and drowned because there was no flow of water through its gills.

I heard of a similar experience which happened to a seventy-three-year-old man who went fishing for tuna off Gloucester Harbour, in Massachusetts. He was taken for such a long ride that his relatives eventually had to call the Coast Guard. They did not succeed in finding him, but the next day a lobster fisherman saw him sitting in his small boat, no less than thirty miles from where the tuna had been hooked. The old man was exhausted, but not at all harmed.

Apparently the tuna had zigzagged with him up and down the coast, but he did not worry about being lost because he recognized the lighthouses along the shore. He found that the boat was too light to tire the fish and realized that if he did not set it free, it could probably go on indefinitely, although there was a chance of its towing him back to Gloucester.

As he told the story he said, "The thing that hurt me most was cutting the line and watching the big rascal flip his tail in defiance as he swam away!"

The coast where this happened is a very fruitful one for tuna fishing. In fact it eventually outdid Wedgeport, for in 1940 a tuna of $8\frac{1}{4}$ hundredweight, which surpassed the Wedgeport record, was taken off Plum Island, Newburyport.

While tuna fishing was developed at Wedgeport, fishing for swordfish was becoming popular off Louisburg, farther up the coast. Now a fisherman could divide his time between two kinds of formidable opponents. Naturally, when we gathered in the evenings to exchange stories, many would be told about our encounters with swordfish.

The swords which these fish are famous for (really elongations of their upper jaws) are so strong that they can cause severe damage to boats and men. One fishing schooner I heard of was so badly damaged by a swordfish that it had to dock at Sydney, Nova Scotia, for major repairs. What happened was that the schooner's crew had been swordfishing off Cape Breton Island when a large fish was sighted by the lookout. The schooner was manœuvred near the fish to allow a good shot with a harpoon.

But the dart failed to strike it in a vital spot. In its rage the swordfish swirled round and drove straight at the vessel's side. Its sword went right through the boat's two-and-a-half-inch-thick planking and snapped off near the fish's head.

Away the swordless fish rushed, but determined to take revenge, the crew pursued it—crippled as their boat was—until it was harpooned and brought aboard. The sword had made such a gaping hole in the side of the boat, that as the boat gradually filled up, it was just able to creep into the harbour.

Another near-shipwreck by a swordfish took place when the fisherman who harpooned it from a large boat jumped into a smaller boat to which the harpoon line was attached. He expected to be towed away by the struggling fish, just as the tuna I described, which are harpooned in the same way, towed away their captors.

But the fish unexpectedly rose to the surface, thrashed around for a few minutes, and charged directly at the boat at full speed. Luckily the man jumped to the thwarts just in time, for the sword went right through the planks. It could have inflicted a serious wound on him.

For about ten minutes there was a terrible commotion on the water as the fish frantically rocked the boat in an effort to get free and the man clung to the thwarts for his life. Eventually the crew of the larger boat came to his rescue and cut off the sword near the head with an axe. This swordless fish, too, was finally boated and taken to market.

Another hazard of Nova Scotia sports fishing (not to speak of many other places) is the presence of sharks. Many a tuna has been half eaten by a shark before it could be boated, and many a fisherman has taken his revenge by landing the shark as well as the tuna.

Commercial fishermen are always ready to tell a hair-raising shark story. Two of my acquaintances, for instance, will never forget what happened when they were trawling in a small boat for halibut off Yarmouth. They were pulling in their trawl lines, taking each fish off the hook as it came up, when one of them leaned over the side to bring in a particularly large halibut. A great white shark with wide open mouth suddenly charged at the halibut in high gear.

Missing its target, the gaping mouth rushed on and struck the small boat right in the centre, with such an impact that both men nearly fell overboard. They wasted no time in seizing the oars and rowing back to the main ship from which they were working; the shark followed them ominously, but they reached the ship in time. The shark's teeth left deep gashes on the side of the boat—a reminder of a very close shave.

I heard another story about a Wedgeport fisherman who was standing on his boat's "pulpit", or harpooning platform, to look for tuna. His mate at the helm also kept watch, and when they saw a commotion on the water, he brought the boat near enough for a good shot.

As the harpooner stood with his weapon raised, a bulky form leaped out of the water straight at him. With a tremendous *crack* it struck the braces supporting the platform and, missing the harpooner by a few inches, fell back into the water. The man was nearly thrown overboard, but he managed to grip the rail until the mate could come to his aid.

When they examined the braces they were horrified to find on them not only the marks of a shark's mouth, but several teeth which it had left in the wood when it struck with such force. The harpooner was so shaken by the incident that he never went after tuna again. In fact, he took to farming. He still keeps the shark's teeth as a grim souvenir.

As we told stories like this during our evenings at Wedgeport, we reflected soberly on the risks which sports fishing involved. But none of us would have missed our Wedgeport experiences for the world. We would always be grateful to Michael Lerner, whose pioneering had made them possible, and who still came every year to Wedgeport to keep up his fight with the great fish. By now his fishing trips were wide-ranging, since he had become an executive of the American

Museum of Natural History, which he frequently supplied with specimens.

One evening he told us about an expedition off the coast of Peru, where he tried a new kind of angling—fishing for giant squid with a rod and reel. He found that they could be hooked easily and played like other deep-water fish. But it was difficult to boat them because they tend to sound (dive suddenly and deeply) and are then attacked by other squid.

The squid is related to the octopus, and its family name, Cephalopoda, is derived from two Greek words meaning "head" and "foot". The feet, or tentacles, of the squid, which has no spine, surround and are actually part of the head. It can swim forward or in reverse equally well. Off the eastern coast of the United States the squid is rather small, but where Lerner was fishing it grows as long as thirty feet and has been known to attack whales.

During the day the squid hides in the depths of the sea, and during the night it rises. Since it is regarded as very good food by many other fish, nature has provided it with one very effective form of protection—the ability to squirt out a stream of a thick, dark, inky substance when an enemy approaches.

When the angler tries to boat a squid, he usually gets a stream of the murky liquid right in his face. Lerner was never to be outdone, however, and he invented a novel fishing costume: a pillowcase over the head with slits in it for his eyes!

The stories of Lerner and others, and of course my own fishing experiences, made my life at Wedgeport a zestful one. But I was always ready for more adventure, and during the winters when there were no tuna and no fishermen at Wedgeport, I took expeditions elsewhere.

10

Exploring with Vanderbilt

THE most exciting trip which I took during the off-season at Wedgeport was a second expedition with George Vanderbilt. But just before this trip I spent some very interesting weeks in Jamaica and Haiti.

In 1936 after the first Wedgeport summer I went to Jamaica for a week to look over prospects for deep-sea fishing there. In company with my wife and an old fishing companion, Gilbert Drake, I made my survey on a semi-official basis; the Jamaicans, who saw what a success tuna fishing had made of Wedgeport, wanted to know if the fish in their area would bring them similar prosperity. Naturally the local newspapers were exceedingly interested in my opinions of the possibilities. As I look back at the clippings, it seems as if I must have spent more time talking to reporters than I did fishing!

But we did find big fish around Jamaica almost at once. The day after our arrival I played, but lost, a marlin which must have weighed nearly 2½ hundredweight. During the succeeding days we hooked several more marlin—a thorough proof that game fishing was a strong possibility for Jamaica waters.

From Jamaica, instead of heading back home, Gilbert Drake and I went on to Haiti, where we had heard there were more marlin to be had. Marlin usually abound in May and June, but we had a feeling that they would be plentiful even at this late date, in October.

When we disembarked with all our fishing tackle at Cap Haitien, we drew a great deal of attention from the Customs inspectors and the loafers around the docks. Since the popula-

tion spoke French and we spoke English, we were forced to
draw pictures of marlin, with their long bills, in an effort to
make ourselves understood.

But we weren't understood anyhow, for the natives had
never heard of marlin. They spoke only of enormous sharks
which in the past few years had devoured six people right in
the harbour.

Mad as we foreigners obviously seemed to them, however,
the islanders and local businessmen were generous with their
help. The steamboat company which had brought us to Haiti
very kindly loaned us a launch. We took with us a native
skipper and a man, known only as José, who was famous as
the island's best fisherman.

Despite their disbelief in our sanity the natives watched with
interest while we lashed a plank across the cockpit of the
launch to serve as a fishing chair, cut several long bamboo
canes for outriggers, and set off for the deep water beyond
the 100-fathom mark, which we knew from experience the
marlins like.

The islanders who were with us told that no one ever
fished so far out; we were wasting our time. When we ran out
our bait from the outriggers, they couldn't contain themselves
any longer and laughed out loud. At this point we weren't
too confident ourselves, and after we had trolled for three
hours without seeing a single movement near our bait, we were
even less confident. The natives began wishing anxiously
to get back to port before we decided to troll right over to
Africa.

Just as we were beginning to think of turning back ourselves, a marlin took my bait. Within a few seconds I was
playing it for all I was worth, and although I eventually lost
it, I gained the admiration of the crew.

In a few minutes we had another strike; this time we landed
a 2¼-hundredweight marlin. It was the only one we got that
day, but we were assured that it was the first which had ever
been caught in that area. We took it back to the town, where
practically the whole population turned out to look at it and
taste pieces. José showed his importance by telling the others

what had happened in long speeches. He seemed to collect a good deal of reflected glory.

The following week we fished every day, boated four marlin, and played several more. We had not only the satisfaction of knowing that the Haitian waters are full of marlin, but the enjoyment of having won the admiration and respect of the natives. As we boarded the steamer to go home they gave us a tremendous send-off.

But I did not have much time to mull over a project completed. At home I began immediately to prepare for the scientific expedition to the Pacific with George Vanderbilt. After our trip on the *White Shadow* in 1931 Vanderbilt had become very interested in the Academy of Natural Sciences in Philadelphia. He found that the Academy would be very glad to have an extensive collection of fish and animals from certain Pacific islands. Intending to combine this collecting task with a pleasant cruise and some sports fishing, Vanderbilt chartered the 168-foot schooner *Cressida* and planned the expedition.

I joined a party which consisted of Vanderbilt and his recent bride Lucille Parsons, who proved to be as earnest an explorer as he; two of Mrs. Vanderbilt's relatives, Mr. and Mrs. Samuel Jones; and Ronald W. Smith, a zoologist in charge of animal collections. During the trip Smith kept a very good diary, which was later used by Dr. Henry W. Fowler, Curator of Fish at the Academy, to write up the results of the expedition.

These results were very impressive: we brought back a total of 10,000 preserved fish of 859 separate species. Five of the genera and seventeen of the species we discovered were completely new. The most productive locality was Christmas Island, which yielded 5,000 fish. One of these fish, a large-eyed, spiny-finned, very tiny (1.9 inches) member of the Myctophidae family, I am particularly proud of, for it bears my name. It is called *Macrostoma grayi*—one of the seventeen new species. Other new species discovered were called *vanderbilti*, *lucillae*, and *ronaldi*, in honour of the rest of the expedition.

We had left Miami on January 23rd, 1937, and passed through

the Panama Canal into the Pacific a week later. Here we visited the Pearl Islands, where we had brought the *White Shadow*, and Malpelo Island, which was so desolate and difficult of access that only four known landings had been made before ours. We travelled on to the Galapagos Islands, where I made what was to be the first of three visits; stopped at the Marquesas Islands, the Tuamotus, the Society Islands (including Tahiti), the Line Islands, Christmas and Fanning Islands, and the Hawaiian Islands. There the Vanderbilts remained for a month, while the Joneses and I returned to the United States. It was time for me to be thinking about Wedgeport.

Our trip was a busy one, for in addition to making daily collections Vanderbilt and I fished for sailfish and marlin with considerable success. When we collected during the day, our methods included poisoning small coves and then taking up the fish in hand nets, spear fishing, and trawling with the bottom net. At night our most productive collecting was done less vigorously with an underwater light. The fish named after me was taken in this way.

Each stop-over had its own wonderful surprise. At the seldom-visited Malpelo Island, where we caught a great variety of fish and several sharks, we discovered, before finally managing to land, a breathtakingly beautiful cave. The walls were brilliantly coloured rocks, and from the ceiling, which was more than one hundred feet high, were suspended stalactites of fantastic shapes.

When we reached the Galapagos Archipelago, which consists of twelve large and hundreds of small islands off the coast of Ecuador, and is managed by the Ecuadorian government, we were struck by the friendliness of the sea lions, who congregate in the bays by the hundreds. Even when we came fairly close, to observe them in their large groups on rocks near very deep water, they did not retreat. The reason for this must be that they don't see human beings often enough to fear them.

They do suffer great depredations, however, from the attacks of orca, or killer whales, and the larger sharks. These voracious creatures patrol the entrances to the bays where the sea lions live, for they know that sooner or later some of them will be tempted to seek food farther out. When this happens, the sea becomes stained with blood as the defenceless sea lions are torn to pieces.

Despite the large population of these friendly creatures, the islands are wild and dreary and extremely lonely. Lavapermeated earth shows that volcanoes have erupted quite recently. Mangroves grow in only a few places. But scientists have long been interested in the islands because much of their life is found nowhere else in the world. At a particular stage in the earth's evolution, it is argued, the islands must have been cut off from the mainland, and this separation preserved forms of life which evolved differently. A huge species of land turtle, for example, which reaches an enormous size and is now becoming very rare, gave the islands their name. And Charles Darwin, who found here several special kinds of Galapagos finches, used them in his research for *The Origin of the Species*.

Now that communications have improved, the population of the Galapagos has probably grown, but when we called, there were about a thousand inhabitants. This was a suitably isolated background for the drama of jealousy and suspicion, ending in probable murder, which a great many newspapers headlined in the early thirties. What we knew about the story attracted our imagination so much that we tried to find out more about it.

The scene of the trouble was Charles Island (called Floreana in Spanish), which is south-east of Albemarle Island, the largest of the Archipelago, and cut off from close contact with other islands. There are only two places on it where it is possible to land—Black Beach and the famous Postoffice Bay. Beside this bay is a large barrel where both inhabitants and ships deposit letters for the outside world. It is the custom for every ship coming by Charles Island to pick up any mail in the barrel for its next port and to leave any of its own mail which can be taken by a ship going in a different direction. A ship will pay to have someone else's mail stamped at port because it knows that another boat will pay for its own. Such informal arrangements are often part of seagoing life. On the *Cressida*, therefore, we dutifully picked up mail and left our own; it was delivered to its destination two and a half months later. The system does work, although a little more slowly than air mail.

To Charles Island at the beginning of 1930 came two Germans, Dr. Frederick Ritter and Miss Dore Strauch. Miss Strauch later collaborated on a book about the subsequent events which was called *Satan Came to Eden* and was published in Germany in 1936.

Dr. Ritter professed extraordinary beliefs about the spiritual life and how it should be attained. A fanatic who took any theory to its logical conclusion, he strongly influenced Miss Strauch, who was then married to a man much older than she. In fact he impressed upon her the need to be alone with him out of the ordinary world in a place where they might attain "spiritual perfection". Dr. Ritter left his wife, Miss Strauch left her husband, and they set off. But before they left, they introduced Frau Ritter to Miss Strauch's husband, so that she could keep house for him!

When they got to Floreana, they had to build a house and start housekeeping from scratch; a slow and painful process it was. There were many wild pigs, asses and cattle on the island, but since Dr. Ritter's principles forbade him to touch meat, they had to cultivate plants. They moved inland to a place they called Friedo and struggled for many weeks to bring up their supplies along the dangerous lava paths from Postoffice Bay. Miss Strauch fell and badly wounded her leg, and many of their supplies were stolen by fishermen who passed the islands. They were forced to leave a note in the mail barrel asking for help from any passing ship.

Help came at the cost of a revealed hide-way. The captain of the ship which gave them medical and other supplies wired the strange story of their existence to newspapers in New York.

Before long reporters were making expeditions to find them; their solitude had only lasted for five months. Among their

many visitors was Vincent Astor, a relation of John Jacob
Astor, who came in 1932. So many invading reporters falsified
the details of their lives that they finally submitted their own
articles.

With the visitors came settlers. The captain of the ship
which brought supplies to the islands from Guayaquil, Ecuador, set up a fishing business in Postoffice Bay. He was fairly
successful for a while, until he drowned off Isabella Island as
his boat broke up against the heavy waves. Five young
Germans, fleeing the beginnings of the Nazi régime, settled
near the bay but did not last long.

In 1932 the Wittmer family arrived and set up house by
the bay near some caves. The family consisted of Herr
Wittmer, his thirteen-year-old son, and his pregnant second
wife. In the same year the Baroness von Wagner-Bousquet also
arrived. Her party included a man called Philippson, whom
she referred to as her husband, and another called Lorenz,
who was known to be in love with her.

The stage was now set for the tragedy. The Baroness immediately antagonized the earlier residents by trying to take
over the island as her property; she even forbade certain ships
to land. Her ideas of exploiting the island as a resort, of building a hotel, disturbed the others, who had come to Floreana
to escape civilization. Worst of all, she set out, according to
Miss Strauch, to entice any man who came within her orbit.
With the captain of one of the vessels which frequently called
at the island she produced a movie, in which she starred as
"Queen of the Galapagos".

In the early part of 1933 Mrs. Wittmer gave birth to the
first native of Floreana, and there was a brief period of peace
between the warring elements. But the passions which usually
boiled on this barren island would not simmer for long.
Jealousy and spite broke out again, as the Baroness "borrowed" animals and beat them, told lies to crews of visiting
ships, and, apparently, stole supplies from the residents which
she sold back to them at exorbitant prices. Her two male
companions, moreover, became murderously jealous of each
other. Lorenz took to visiting Dr. Ritter and Miss Strauch,

whose privacy was sadly shattered, to tell them tales of his distress.

Then another lover turned up. He was badly injured in a shooting accident, during which the Baroness was evidently aiming at still another young man. The latter she hoped to injure very slightly so that she would have a chance to put him under her spell before he left the island. Small wonder that Dr. Ritter and Miss Strauch felt the world was pursuing them!

On March 19, 1934, the recluses heard from their self-built home at Friedo a terrible scream, and then silence. The Baroness and Philippson were never seen again. Some time later both Lorenz and the Wittmers, who were neighbours of the Baroness and shared a water supply with her, came to visit Friedo with a very suspicious tale. They said the Baroness and Philippson had embarked on a yacht which had called to take them to the South Sea Islands. Miss Strauch firmly believed that Lorenz had murdered both of them, for when she visited the Baroness's home there were no signs of the departure he had described. The Wittmers remained silent.

The truth was never discovered, for Lorenz soon left the island in a boat which was wrecked on a rocky shore near Chatham Island. His skeleton and the skeleton of the boat's owner were later found in positions which showed that they died of thirst in great agony. Lorenz's secret died with him, and the bodies of the Baroness and Philippson were never found.

In November, 1934, Dr. Ritter died of a mysterious illness, and Miss Strauch returned to Germany. The Wittmers were left in sole possession of both the island and the mystery.

It was with this knowledge that we landed at Postoffice Bay, and like most ships which went through the Galapagos, we tried to find the Wittmers. We searched for three days, found only the deserted house of Dr. Ritter and Miss Strauch, and lost three of our crew overnight. A little later on we encountered a boat which had stopped at the island earlier, and the captain declared that he had found the Wittmers then. Evidently they still lived there, but must have been in some other part of the island when we arrived.

This was by no means the end of my interest in the Floreana tragedy, although nothing more was revealed on this expedition.

From the Galapagos we struck right across the Pacific to the Marquesas Islands, where we discovered that the population, which only seventy-five years ago used to be about ten thousand, now numbers less than three thousand. Conditions were primitive. But at Takaroa in the Tuamotus we saw several Fords, numerous bicycles, half a mile of road, and a village of about three hundred, some of whom we hired to help us in our spear fishing. Generally speaking, I found life in the South Sea Islands shabby and uncivilized—no paradise despite the palm trees and the blue lagoons.

On the island of Bora-Bora in the Society Archipelago we watched the natives enjoying what is known as "stone fishing". It is basically the same as the tarpon fishing of the San Blas Indians, but instead of the stakes which the Indians use, the Bora-Bora natives use a trap constructed of stones and coral. In both groups the entire population of a village takes part.

When the chief of a Bora-Bora village sets the day for a stone fishing ceremony, all the men, women, and children, shining brown-skinned in the sun and dressed gaily in the bright clothes they are famed for, throng to the shore. At the shallow end of a lagoon, which surrounds so many of the Southern Pacific islands, they make the trap. Here is an ideal fishing place, because the barrier reef of coral which forms the lagoon stands a little distance from the mainland and breaks the force of the huge waves.

After building the circle of stones and coral, into whose funnel-shaped entrance the fish will be driven, the natives gather on the shore for a ceremony of prayers to their ancient gods.

Then the men load their canoes with palm fronds and paddle down the lagoon for about a mile. There they leave the canoes, stretch across the lagoon in a great line with the palm fronds between them, and driving the fish ahead of them, wade to the trap. Besides using the palm fronds there is another method of frightening the fish into swimming the right way. The stronger men stir up the water by swinging ropes of plaited palm fibres with five-pound stones on the end. It is this commotion with stones that gives the ritual its name,

As the line approaches the trap, it doubles and shortens. and the gaps are gradually closed. Although some of the men have to give up with exhaustion, the fish have no chance of escaping.

At last they are all forced into the circle of stones, where they will now be speared for the feast. Custom demands that if a distinguished visitor is present, he shall be asked to spear the first fish. When we were present this distinction fell to Vanderbilt, who took advantage of it with great enthusiasm.

As soon as he waded out of the water, the village plunged in with equal enthusiasm. As is usual, it frenziedly kept at the job until the very last fish was caught. Then, as is also usual, the fish were divided equally among the population. They were borne triumphantly to be eaten at a huge meal or dried for future use.

Another kind of fishing, which we discovered in the Cook Islands, is similar to our method of poisoning a small pool. The main difference is that the islanders use a poison which does not affect the value of the fish as food.

In the native language their practice is called "ora". It represents a whole day's work. About a dozen people comb the jungle in search of a tree whose botanical name is *Barringtonia speciosa*. This tree carries a large squash-like fruit about the size of an orange, and inside each fruit is a single seed. When the party gathers at a chosen spot, the seeds are removed and crushed into a pulpy and poisonous paste. The paste is put into bags made from plaited palm fronds.

After eating a specially prepared picnic lunch, the fishermen load their bags of paste and other equipment into canoes. Paddling out to the barrier reefs which separate the lagoon from the sea, they arrive at ebb tide so that the reefs will be well out of water. In the reefs the tide leaves a number of very shallow pools, often two or three acres in area, which house many varieties of fish.

The women of the party drag the sacks of paste across each

pool until it is well polluted with the poisonous substance which seeps from the bags. The poison has the effect of stupefying the fish, which rise to the surface or swim slowly and aimlessly. After it has had a little time to work its full effect, the men enter the pool and collect whatever fish they require.

Many other creatures besides food fish are paralysed. Moray eels, octopuses, and sea scorpions come floating to the surface as they lose their hold on rock or bottom. But although the fishermen leave unconscious fish which they do not use, their destruction is not as great as you might think. The young and small fish all die, but the larger and stronger ones are often saved by the incoming tide, which floods the pools with clean, pure water.

A more potent poison, more wasteful of fish, is used by the natives of the Philippines, who make a mash of the seeds of the *Croton tiglium* tree and perform much the same actions as the Bora-Bora natives. In many Pacific islands and South America the roots of a small woody vine called *Derris elliptica* are also used for poisoning. In this case the crushed roots are simply thrown into a pool, and everything is killed as the poison takes effect. Some of the Panama Indians, who like the San Blas Indians are very wide-ranging sailors, affix wads of the *Derris elliptica* to their cayugas or canoes; they believe that if they capsize in the ocean, the poison will keep the sharks away. It would be very difficult to prove the efficacy of this precaution.

After learning about poisoning in the Cook Islands, we continued north to Christmas and Palmyra Islands and then headed for Honolulu. On the way to Honolulu we had hoped to have some sports fishing, but since there was a hurricane in the Pacific at the time, the weather was too bad for us to do anything but try to make headway. We were three days behind schedule in sighting the Hawaiian Islands, and by the time we arrived the ship's supplies were very short. Water, particularly, was down to a few bottles.

This situation led to a plan of action which caused a great deal of fuss in the newspapers; a misunderstanding made it appear as if Vanderbilt were trying to evade the Customs officers. In fact the collector of Customs levied against the

I am displaying the world's record sailfish, which I caught almost one-handed.

(*right*) These terrifying teeth belong to a great white shark, known as the only true man-eating shark.

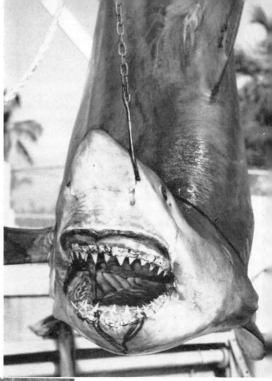

(*Photos: courtesy UPI*)

(*left*) This tiger shark has just been hooked from a Seaquarium collecting boat.

(*above*)　A needlefish larger than the one which unintentionally attacked me.

(*below*)　Demonstrating the barracuda's striking power.

(*Photos: courtesy the Seaquarium*)

(*above*) " Eyes " on the underside of sawfish are really air holes; true eyes are on top.

(*below*)   The remora shark, with suction plate on top of its head.

The rare moray eel.

(Photo: courtesy the Seaquarium)

(*above*) Taken at Wedge-port with a rod and line, these tuna weigh a total of twenty-two hundredweight. John Manning, subsequent holder of a world's record for tuna, is at the left.

(*right*) Johnnie and Archie Cass were among the first to fight giant bluefins off Bimini. The bluefin they have landed here was mangled by a shark.

(*left*) The tarpon I am hoisting died en route to Marine Studios. Notice its large scales.

(*Photo: courtesy Marine Studios*)

(*below*) This lemon shark, entangled in porpoise nets off Turtle Mound, had to be tied to a tree.

(*above*) My favourite picture of the whale shark shows its markings clearly.

(*below*) The orca, or killer whale, is recognised by its prominent dorsal fin.

master of the *Cressida* a large fine which was not remitted until
full explanation was made.

What had happened was this: the bad weather and our lack
of water caused us such discomfort that when we were about
thirty-six miles away from Honolulu, Vanderbilt asked our
captain to radio the Honolulu Customs and Immigration
officials for permission to land that night from a launch we
carried aboard the boat. Permission was granted, and when we
arrived in Honolulu we were not met by the usual group of
Customs officials. Since we carried no baggage, we did not feel
the need to do anything but find a comfortable hotel.

The Press, lured by Vanderbilt's name, made inquiries and
got hold of the wrong end of the story. Their stories assumed
that Vanderbilt had arrived in defiance of the Customs. It was
some time before the proper officials could be found and the
whole matter straightened out.

Leaving the Vanderbilts and the *Cressida* in Honolulu, I
returned home. I was already catching tuna in Nova Scotia on
July 18, when the *Cressida* arrived in New York with all our
specimens aboard. From here they were shipped to Philadelphia to be classified, and a full report of them was later
published in the Academy's monograph series.

In the following years Vanderbilt organized three more
expeditions, but because of other commitments I was unable
to go. It was not until his fifth expedition in 1941 that I was
able to sail with him. This time we visited Caribbean, Western
Pacific, and Mexican islands. Except for the zoologist Ronald
Smith, whose place was taken by an ornithologist aptly named
Dawson Feathers, all the *Cressida* collectors were aboard.

We sailed on Vanderbilt's 172-foot, 327-ton *Pioneer*, a
special expedition yacht whose equipment included a large
refrigerator for skinned birds. Disembarking from the
Bahamas, where we collected many fish from the islands and
keys, we sailed through the Panama Canal to the Pearl Islands
and the coast of Colombia, and revisited the Galapagos. Instead
of striking across the Pacific, as we had done the last time, we
cruised up the Mexican coast to the Revilla Gigedo and the
Tres Marias Islands and landed at San Pedro, California.

In late April, 1941, while we were based on San Miguel Bay on the Darien coast of Pacific Panama, we pioneered the ascent of Cerro del Sapo to get some birds from the summit. First we made an aerial survey from Balboa, which seemed to show that a landing on a particularly high beach would provide the best access. But when we landed at the beach, we saw that from that point an ascent was impossible. We had to sail round Garachine Point, land there, and make a very long climb. After hewing trails out of solid jungle all the way up, we finally established a base camp on the mountain's shoulder. This, we hoped, would make things easier for any other collectors who followed us in the region.

We nearly lost the birds which had cost so much labour to acquire when the yacht's generators broke down off the coast of Mexico later in the trip. Abandoning our planned route, we rushed to Acapulco for repairs and luckily were able to save the birds.

While we were still in Panama, Vanderbilt and I went in for a new sort of night lighting. Previously when our intention had been to attract fish, we had shone the light under water. But since our quarry this time was small birds and reptiles, we decided to swing a big beam from side to side. If something we wanted as a specimen were drawn within the circle of the light, we would kill it with a shotgun. But we both obeyed a rigid rule: never kill anything unnecessarily.

We set off for our experiment in a skiff with an outboard motor up one of the small rivers which make lace of the Pacific Panama shore. In the beautiful jungle night the tangled vegetation overhung the dark water. We went quite far upstream and then waited for full darkness so that we could drift back downstream without using the motor. Absolute silence was essential if we were not to frighten the animals.

As we began to drift, shining the light at the shores, the eyes of many animals reflected like twin lamps in the dense black of the forest. The scene was weird and a little frightening. Suddenly we noticed that ahead of us was an animal which appeared to have only one eye; only one huge reflection was visible as we shone the light at it. What could it possibly be?

Vanderbilt and I began to wonder if we would return to the United States with a rare and marvellous beast.

But since we had never heard of any one-eyed creatures, we decided to shoot it first and see what it was later. Vanderbilt, shotgun in hand, sat in the prow of the skiff as I paddled it quietly to within range. When we were about thirty yards away, he aimed and fired. The light went out.

The sound of that shot, which echoed round and round the valley, started a huge commotion among the jungle animals. Howler monkeys made every sort of noise from a scream to a moan; parrots and macaws rasped and squawked, and unidentified creatures screeched. For some time afterwards we were both frightened.

After the noise subsided a little, we investigated what we had caught. Approaching the spot where we had seen the eye reflect, we found a long spit of sand projecting from the shore. We reasoned that our catch must be somewhere on the sand, but from the boat we couldn't see a thing—certainly nothing large enough to have an eye of the size we had seen. Bewildered, we brought the boat up on the sand and stepped out to look; perhaps, we thought, the creature had only been wounded and had crawled away.

We still found nothing, until we shone the light directly on the spot where the full charge of shot had hit the sand. There, right in the pattern left by the shot, lay the dead body of a twelve-inch crocodile!

Our hopes of a one-eyed monster dissolved in hoots of laughter. From that time on we remembered that the eyes of baby crocodiles, because they are so close together, look like one ball of light when they reflect. We never again tried to shoot when we saw only one eye.

After we had stopped laughing and the jungle had settled into silence (fortunately this didn't take too long), we continued our collecting of genuine specimens. We returned to the *Pioneer* just before daybreak and probably, although I do not remember, went off for more specimens soon afterwards. Such a timetable would be quite likely, since on an expedition no one gets any sleep.

I do remember—with horrible and terrifying vividness—
that our next major adventure took place when we revisited
the Galapagos. After stopping briefly at each of the islands in
turn, we spent two days on Albermarle Island off Tagus Cove.
It was here that we had an encounter with the orcas, or killer
whales.

These whales are particularly frightening because they live
on the flesh of other mammals. They are never much longer
than sixteen feet, but because they hunt in packs they are a
menace to creatures several times their size. A typical pack of
ten will kill an eighty- or ninety-foot whale in less than an
hour; with their conical teeth they will seize it by the lips and
tear at the mouth to get at the tongue—a special delicacy.
Orcas do not confine their killings to other whales, but attack
porpoises, sea lions, and seals whenever they find them. Their
voracity is well-illustrated by the results of an autopsy which
was performed on an orca taken off the coast of British Colum-
bia. Inside its stomach were the remains of thirteen porpoises
and fourteen seals. Luckily orcas are not plentiful, and when
they do appear they advertise their presence with high dorsal
fins, which cut through the water like small black sails.

One day when Vanderbilt and I were out in the *Pioneer*'s
launch, we saw eight or ten of these orcas slaughtering a group
of sea lions. Since we had noticed on our previous expedition
to the Galapagos that its large sea lion population was exceedingly tame, we were not surprised to see, as we approached,
that the orcas were cutting the helpless creatures to shreds.
Splotches of blood were staining the blue water.

Vanderbilt, at the controls of the launch, urged me to spear
one of the whales. I took a harpoon and stood on the platform
of the boat. But looking down at those vicious creatures, I lost
my nerve; when I saw that,one of them had an eye as big as a
grapefruit, my arm froze.

I asked Vanderbilt to bring the boat alongside a smaller
orca, but again I lost my nerve. I purposely missed the shot.
My fear was, I think, that if I harpooned the whale and he took
me in tow, I might fall into the water and be torn to pieces like
the sea lions. After another try I had to confess to Vanderbilt

that I was completely terrified. When he took another look at the dorsal fins quickly whipping through the water as they turned this way and that, he at once turned the helm away from the scene.

When we returned to the *Pioneer*, still shaking from the horror of what we had seen, the captain of the yacht told us that we had been wise to leave the pack of orcas, especially since they were on a killing expedition. He told us about three men who ran into a pack of killer whales when they were in a small boat like ours. The orcas turned on the boat and smashed it with their powerful jaws; neither boat nor men were ever seen again, despite the fact that the big ship from which the men were launched was only 200 yards away. The rest of the crew just watched helplessly.

I felt we had had a narrow escape.

When we got back to the United States after this expedition, we had 5,787 fish, 863 of which came from the Caribbean Sea and the rest from the Pacific coast of Panama and the Mexican islands. The Caribbean yielded 167 species and the Pacific 456 species. This expedition was especially productive of unknown fish: no less than twenty-seven new genera or subgenera and sixty new species or subspecies.

Again a new species was named after me. This time it was a variant of a completely new subgenus, the *Spinipercina*; my fish is called *Spinipercina grayi*. It is, I'm afraid, an even smaller fish than the other one named after me, for it is only eight-tenths of an inch long. It is a dark olive-brown and has very spiny fins and spiky gill-covers. We found it by night-lighting off the Pearl Islands, which are a fitting locality for a fish bearing my name because I have always loved them since my visit in 1931. And to give one's name to a new creature—what better form of immortality for a life-long collector?

11

The Carola *Among the Galapagos*

L EON MANDEL, whom I had met in the early thirties, was
one of the earliest anglers to try his hand against tuna at
Wedgeport. He was also one of the most successful. He
and I became great friends, for when we talked and listened in
the evenings to tales about fishing, we discovered that we had
the same enthusiasm for collecting wild-life rather than killing
it for sport.

After George Vanderbilt organized his first expedition in
1937, Mandel realized, as Vanderbilt had, that here was a very
pleasurable way to combine interests in sport and natural
history. Mandel contacted the Field Museum of Chicago, now
called the Chicago Museum of Natural History, and began
to make arrangements with the staff to organize a collecting
expedition for specimens. Pressure of business, however, prevented any further developments until 1939, when, after the
Wedgeport tuna season, Mandel asked me to join him as collecting director on an expedition to the lower Caribbean and
the western part of the Gulf of Mexico.

Aboard Mandel's luxurious yacht, the *Buccaneer*, we spent
a few weeks collecting and preserving fish for the museum.
We also took a number of birds and reptiles off the islands.

This trip was really a pilot venture. When Mandel and the
museum found it was very much worth the effort and expense,
they decided to organize a much more extensive one to the
Galapagos. For this purpose a new yacht, the *Carola*, was
bought and fitted out. It was named to honour Mandel's wife,
who accompanied us on the expedition and proved to be a
first-class fisherwoman and collecting assistant. Because she

was particularly useful in shooting rare birds, we were not surprised when she later became the United States women's skeet-shooting champion. In addition to these accomplishments she possesses a keen sense of fashion; she is annually on the list of America's best dressed women.

The *Carola*, which was practically an ocean liner in its appointments, left Jacksonville, Florida, on December 19th, 1940, went through the Panama Canal, stopped at nearly every island in the Galapagos, visited Talara on the coast of Peru, and stopped at Cocos Island off Costa Rica before returning through the canal to dock at New Orleans on March 10th, 1941. There were eleven of us in the collecting party, including seven scientists from the Field Museum who took the entire trip and another who joined us in Talara for the return journey. The crew consisted of thirty-three men and one woman, who was stewardess for Mrs. Mandel.

This expedition produced not only a vast number of very valuable specimens, but a delightful literary souvenir in the form of a composite diary. Each of eight members of the party wrote up one day's activities and on the next day read to the others what he had written. This provided a great deal of amusement when various members objected to what had been imputed to them. On two days, Mrs. Mandel wrote up the contribution of Rudyerd Boulton, an ornithologist and photographer, in exchange for his promise to get her a baby sea lion for a pet. This he later did, but unfortunately the baby would not feed and died. The diary was published privately in Chicago by Mandel later in 1941.

Another diversion was sports fishing—especially for marlin. Mandel was especially interested in marlin because never in his long angling career had he taken one. He had heard that they were to be found in abundance off the Galapagos and the coasts of Peru and Chile.

He was absolutely sure that he could catch a marlin, or some other big fish, from a boat the size of the *Carola*. The rest of us told him that this was not possible; at best he would lose five or six hundred yards of line before the fast boat could be slowed down enough to play the fish. I felt that he could not even hook a marlin at the *Carola*'s speed; it would be much more sensible to go after game fish from one of the small boats we had aboard, such as the *Carola Junior*. But Mandel was determined to use the yacht.

He had rigged up a fishing chair in the stern and had devised a system of wires, with a buzzer attached, which ran from his position to the pilot house. If he were to hook a fish, he could communicate to the captain the course he wanted the yacht to take in pursuit. He and the captain worked out an elaborate set of wire-buzzing signals, which no one, except Mandel, expected to be used.

On January 16th we had cleared the Panama Canal and were enjoying our first day on the Pacific. We had set a straight course from Balboa to the Galapagos and were cruising at about thirteen knots. Not many of us were doing anything in particular except looking at the blue water; the régime of long days and short nights with little sleep had not yet set in.

I set up Mandel's heavy fishing rod and dropped a white-feather-bait into the water behind the stern at a suitable trolling distance. Mandel adjusted his shoulder harness, gripped the rod, and leaned back in his chair to enjoy a sun bath. I lounged against the rail, enjoying the scenery with the rest of the party.

I was startled by Mandel's sudden yell, "Strike!" It was only a matter of minutes since we had sent out the bait, and I couldn't believe my ears. But behind the stern there it was— a marlin lunging at the white feather. After a few angry passes he caught the lure and the hook set. The fish took off at right-angles, nearly jerking Mandel out of his chair.

The buzzer began its series of signals, and as the fish changed its tactics, the boat slowed down, turned, swung, stopped, started. The catch was so entirely unexpected that the captain, who could not see the part of the stern where the fishing chair was located, thought the whole thing was a rehearsal of the signals. He went on following them in the spirit of the game and was very surprised to find, when he stepped out of the pilot house for a moment, that Mandel actually had a marlin.

The excitement on board was infectious; everyone was dashing for cameras and scurrying to the rails to watch the fun. One of the scientists added to the confusion by trying to fire three guns at once to deal with any sharks that might attack the marlin. But in spite of the excitement the co-ordination between the fisherman and the pilot house was excellent. The yacht was so skilfully handled that the marlin did not get fouled on its propellers or other parts.

The fighting fish veered from one side of the ship to the other, often taking 500 yards of line before changing his course. He made several leaps and long runs and thrashed angrily on the surface. All these quick manœuvres put the large ship's steering mechanism under more strain than it had probably ever undergone before. Once when the marlin got away from us about seventy-five yards off the bow, it took a quarter of an hour at full speed to get him over to the stern again.

At the end of an hour and a half of fighting, he got tired and as a last resort settled down to deep sounding. I decided to launch the longboat from the deck and, with two sailors, try to land him. Mandel manœuvred the fish near the boat until I was able to take hold of the leader and grab him by the bill. I couldn't actually bring him aboard the longboat, for he was too heavy, but I clung on to him with gloved hands while the two sailors rowed the boat back to the yacht. There he was hoisted to the deck with a block and tackle.

He was a striped marlin weighing 3 hundredweight—a very respectable size and definite proof that Mandel's buzzer system worked. The fish was skinned in order to preserve it, and for dinner the whole party ate marlin steaks, which taste much like the swordfish to which the marlin is related. During the rest of the day and throughout most of the trip we continued to troll from the yacht, but we never again had such luck. After this, marlin, sailfish and tuna were taken, but from the *Carola Junior*, not the big *Carola*.

Three days after the first marlin we dropped anchor off Tower Island in the Galapagos and the serious work of the expedition began. The scientists had three main objects: to collect for the museum some native birds and, for an exhibit of Galapagos under-water life, as many representative fish as possible, and to gather, for scientific data, such miscellaneous local fauna as mice of various kinds. The Mandels also wanted to bring back some animals, particularly the land-turtles which give the Galapagos their name. They planned to put these animals in the Brookfield Zoo in Chicago and a zoo in Havana, of which Mr. and Mrs. Mandel were respective directors.

Throughout the whole expedition the scientists worked tremendously hard. Their tasks did not end, as mine did, when the fish, birds or animals were caught and killed, but included skinning them and preserving them for the homeward journey. One of their problems was that we shot so many birds that they sometimes had trouble keeping up with us. As one of them pointed out, you can shoot more birds in two hours than you can skin in twelve. To finish their preserving, therefore, the scientists frequently stayed up until midnight or later. Then they had to be up in the morning at five or six o'clock to go after more specimens.

In fact our work made all of us keep odd hours. Some days began for half the party at the point where for the other half they ended. One morning, for example, one of the collectors and I were up at 3.45 a.m.—less than half an hour after the late skinning crews had gone to bed. We were after flying fish to be used for bait and hoped to attract them with an underwater light as soon as the moon had gone down. But since the sun came up before the moon disappeared, we were not successful.

Another characteristic feature of our work was its plethora of equipment. The scientists were especially burdened, as Mandel notes in a joking but essentially true description: "A word regarding the light baggage of the collecting scientists might be appropriate. If he goes out only fifty yards, he travels with no less than ten odd khaki-covered boxes. He is also considered *déclassé* if every pocket does not drip with assorted gadgets. Always, when he reaches his collecting spot, he has forgotten between four and fourteen necessities. Naturally, if his trip is longer than fifty yards, the baggage multiplies rapidly."

Some of this baggage, when it was used for all-day trips to

the islands, actually did prove more than necessary. And even more equipment was brought when a few of the scientists made camps for all-night stays in particularly fruitful places.

But our strenuous efforts were certainly rewarding. They produced for the Field Museum a skinned and preserved collection of one thousand fish of one hundred and sixty different species, three hundred and thirty-five small birds, forty large birds, eighty-six lizards, nine marine iguanas, three land iguanas, four snakes, eighteen mice, and the skulls of a porpoise and a sea lion. For distribution to the zoos we brought back alive eleven penguins, three frigate birds, nine Galapagos finches, a pair of albatrosses, four land iguanas and four huge clumsy Galapagos turtles.

Many of our preserved fish were caught by means of the dynamite technique: one of the scientists and I would set off a charge at a spot where we knew there were plenty of the fish we wanted. Since we wanted specimens which were dead, this was the best possible method; the charge would stun or kill the fish without harming their appearance—as hook-and-line or spear fishing might.

We did do some spearing, however, as well as some bottom fishing using a trawl net drawn along the bottom of the ocean. The trawl net collected huge quantities of things we didn't want, as well as those we did.

The scientists also did a great deal of night lighting, and I frequently helped them. One of the most exciting things we caught—by attracting it with a night light and securing it with a dip net—was a five-inch baby sailfish, perfect in every detail and a miniature copy of the adult. This proved that sailfish spawn in the western Pacific and that their young form is exactly the same as that of the older fish. We also caught a five-inch baby dolphin by means of the same technique.

When we were out fishing we were frequently bothered by the sea birds which abound throughout the islands. Frigate birds and boobies would accumulate in great clouds above us as soon as we let out the bait. The birds were so fearless that they would pick up the bait from the water, and then we had to replace it.

The frigate bird or booby has a very good technique for getting itself a meal when there is no fisherman with free bait in the area. It flies over the surface, looking down at the flying fish it is after. When a big fish, such as a shark or tuna, comes up beneath the small flying fish, they usually take to the air to escape. Then the bird comes swooping down and grabs them without even getting wet.

The frigate or booby does not scorn a meal obtained from some other sea bird who has spent a lot of time waiting for fish to break the surface. When the frigate, for example, sees another bird with a fish, it swoops down on it and begins to persecute it. The bird is forced to fly higher and higher to escape the frigate's viciously long beak, and eventually it has to let go of its fish. Immediately the frigate stops pecking at the bird and dives after the fish to catch it before it hits the water.

We tried everything we could to keep the birds away when we were fishing—even capturing a bird and tying a balloon to it to attract the other birds' attention. We also tried giving the birds a free meal by sending out special strips of bait. But it was found that the most effective way of keeping them off was to fire a gun at them, even though this was a little inconvenient from a small boat when I wanted to be fishing.

On one occasion, off Elizabeth Bay, I got a little closer to a large booby than I wanted to, especially since birds were not really my province. I had rashly promised a dinner of crawfish to the whole crew and party—a total of forty-four people—when we got to the bay, which, as I knew from my previous visit, was an excellent place for crawfish. Everyone intended to hold me to my promise, so one night I set out in a small boat with two sailors, intending to spear the crawfish by the light of a gas lamp in the bows.

On the way we saw some penguins perched on the steep rocky ledges of the cliffs and since we always had the main purposes of the expedition in mind, I jumped out and grabbed at them. They were so wary of me that I was forced to crawl into deep cliff caves where I could corner them before I managed to return with about half a dozen.

As we proceeded along the cliffs in the boat, we took many crawfish and some of the fish needed for the museum with spears and nets. One crawfish weighed seven and a half pounds. We also saw many sea lions, for in this part of the world where they are rarely hunted by humans, they are not at all afraid to be seen by them. We passed two great herds near the rocks, brushing against some with a net-handle or an oar, and even this did not disturb them. Cormorants and sea iguanas looked at us from the rocky ledges. It was fascinating to my two companions, and we were all thoroughly enjoying the beauty of the tropical night.

Suddenly, as I was standing in the bow with a spear ready to aim at still another crawfish, I got a terrific blow on the head and went sprawling into the bottom of the boat. The gas lamp went overboard at the same time. I was furiously angry, thinking that for some unknown reason, one of my companions had hit me on the head with an oar. They quieted me down and re-lit the extra lamp, explaining that a big booby had dived right off the cliff directly at the lamp. Instead of getting it, he hit me instead. I was still a little disinclined to believe the story until I saw another booby attempt to put out the light in the same way—this time without hitting me. The force of the booby's dive was amply demonstrated by the size of the bump which the first bird had put on my head.

Later on we had a more peaceful encounter with two albatrosses, destined for the Brookfield Zoo in Chicago, whose capture was more a matter of luck than of scientific judgment. The particular kind of bird we caught, which figures so prominently in Coleridge's poem *The Ancient Mariner*, is called a wandering albatross, for it spends all its life on the wing, landing only to lay its eggs and then begin again its lonely flight over the seas.

Rudyerd Boulton, the ornithologist, who endeared himself to Mrs. Mandel by finding her a baby sea lion and to the rest of the party by his inability to get up early in the mornings, was an expert on the albatross. He told us that one of its few nesting places, where we might be likely to find one, was on Hood Island, the last we were to touch. Since I knew the area well, we set off in a dinghy with the feeling that it would be a simple matter to get our albatross.

When we got to the island, we found it completely barren of any life except for lizards. Scattered about were many cracked egg shells, which proved that we had come too late. The newly-hatched birds were probably flying high above some very distant sea. We went over the whole island, feeling very hopeless, until on the far side we did find one lonely half-grown female. When we approached, it made no effort to fly away, and we soon captured it; we found that it was in perfect condition except for the deformation of one wing, which prevented it from flying with the rest of its brood. I suppose the poor bird almost welcomed capture for the sake of a little company, for it would have otherwise been condemned to a very lonely existence.

We were glad to have one albatross in our improvised zoo on the deck of the *Carola*, but we wanted another. Several days before we were to leave the coast of South America for the homeward trip, we found it—quite by accident. Mandel was trolling for broadbill swordfish off Peru and was having no luck at all. Suddenly a great bird swooped down from the sky, picked up the bait, and was hooked immediately. We were just about to curse the frigate birds again for interfering with our fishing when we realized that what we had caught was an albatross with the markings of a male—just what we needed to complete the pair. We carefully pulled it in and boated it, released it from the painful hook, and put it in the cage with the broken-winged female. Mandel was very elated that he had beaten the collecting scientists at their own game.

Another important find was a giant manta ray, which Mandel and I came upon one afternoon just after we had set out. The collecting crew had decided that what was needed was a manta about ten or twelve feet across, since one larger than this would be difficult to handle. Here, as if made to order, was our specimen; Mandel and I set to with harpoons to secure it. The first harpoon went in easily enough, but it took us about an hour to set in the second. Then we brought the manta to the surface and shot it. We towed it into a cove (with the help of most of the ship's crew and some of the scientists who had been skinning birds on board the *Carola*) and left it there for two of the museum staff to deal with.

It was obvious that such a large creature could not be taken back in its entirety; therefore the two scientists were faced with the task of making a cast of it. This they would take back to the museum and use as a mould to make a model for the exhibit. We left them that night on the shore of the cove so that they could work on the manta without wasting time making trips back and forth from the yacht.

It took the two men a whole day to cast the manta; the casts themselves were so large that they had to be divided into sections for crating. The men spent another night on the beach and proceeded to make, at twelve-inch intervals, a chart of the manta which would help them, when they came to build the model, in keeping correct proportions.

When this tremendous work was all done, when the pieces were crated and stored on the *Carola* and the equipment was cleaned and ready for another big fish, we sent a telegram to Stanley Field asking if a manta of the size we had would be adequate for the museum's needs. Later that evening when we were all at dinner, a radiogram was delivered to the leader of the museum party: "Message received—regret twelve-foot manta entirely inadequate—require at least twenty to twenty-five feet. Exhibition of twelve-foot specimen inadvisable, but large one most desirable—two or three days well worth spending—Stanley Field."

The two men must have felt every ache in their tired bones as they read that radiogram. Not only would we have to catch and cast another manta, but since there was no plaster left on the ship, we would have to visit a post 600 miles away to get some.

But they looked at the radiogram again—and suddenly its not quite correct appearance made them realize it was all a joke. Someone among the party, and they never found out who, had thought up the hoax in connivance with the ship's radio officer; the radiogram was fixed to look as if it had come from Chicago. I'm afraid that we thoroughly enjoyed the scientists' misery.

We had a welcome respite from our arduous collecting chores while we were anchored off Seymour Island, where we visited a very trim-looking clipper, the *American Beauty*. We found out that she was a commercial boat from San Diego, California, and she was fishing for Pacific yellowfin tuna. Since I was vitally concerned with the sports angle of tuna fishing, I was very interested in the methods used by commercial fishermen and was glad of an opportunity to watch their operations. The Portuguese crew was very friendly to us when we came aboard one evening for a tour.

The boat was equipped with a live-well, full of sardines and anchovies used as live bait. When a school of tuna was located, huge quantities of them were thrown overboard; since they are the natural prey of tuna, they all swam close to the ship for protection. This was very important, for in this kind of fishing it was vital to have the tuna near the boat.

Every man on board, including the cook, took a position at the rail. Instead of a fishing rod he used a bamboo pole. His lure, which was a feather dangled on the surface of the water and kept moving, encouraged the tuna to strike at it from beneath. As soon as a tuna took the bait, the fisherman struck his hook into it and heaved his pole up and over his shoulder in one follow-through motion, like a golf-stroke. Because the hooks were not barbed, this quick motion was absolutely necessary if the tuna were to be lifted. Once the tuna was landed in the fishing-well behind the angler, the slacking of the line released the hook so that it did not have to be taken out of the mouth by hand.

This method of fishing meant that a tremendous weight of tuna could be landed in a very short time from a big school. When a fish weighed more than forty pounds, it was caught by two men who had separate poles attached to a single hook; the heaviest fish were caught by three men, all moving in unison. Since the bamboo poles did not yield very much, the fish could not be allowed to get its head down and pull away after it took the bait; otherwise poles and men would land in the water.

When that happened, sharks were the chief menace. Guns were kept handy to scare them off, but unfortunately the guns themselves were something of a danger. On one tuna clipper the skipper accidentally shot one of his men in the shoulder while firing at a shark. Since the wound was not serious, however, and since instructions for dealing with it were radioed to the ship constantly, the man didn't have to be taken ashore. His shoulder healed quickly enough for him to be back heaving his share of the tuna before the end of the trip.

The record catch at that time for a commercial fishing clipper was 113 tons of tuna a day—about five times as much as was caught at Wedgeport during the 1940 season! The *American Beauty*'s record was 70 tons a day; by the time she returned to port after an expedition she would be loaded to the gunwales with a frozen catch of about 330 tons, which filled every inch of storage space. Her crew of seventeen fished on shares, as we had done when we went after bluefish in New Jersey, but the total income from the catch was considerably cut down by the necessity of paying a tax to the Ecuadorian government for fishing in Galapagos waters. Even twenty years ago, when I visited the *American Beauty*, the average tax on the catch was $2,200.

Before we left the Galapagos, we were anxious to find out more about the mysterious Charles Island murders which had so much intrigued us on our previous trip. We asked about the events and the strange people connected with them wherever we found any inhabitants. But we were to come into closer contact with the survivors of those events than we had thought.

On Chatham Island there was a body of water called Wreck Bay in front of the village of Puerto Chico, which appeared to be the Galapagos metropolis, since the governor had his official residence there. Behind the village was the town of Progreso, where there was a hospital and a rather large colony of sugar planters. When we put down anchor at Wreck Bay, the governor came aboard to be entertained by the Mandels, who later went to Puerto Chico to buy some of the native Galapagos dogs.

The next morning, when the *Carola* was still in the bay, a procession of boats bearing Galapagos wild puppies came to the boat and tried to sell them to us. Another boat brought three of the famous Galapagos tortoises, which we took aboard for shipping to zoos. And then came a launch containing a man and a woman.

They called up to the *Carola* that they had nothing to sell but wanted our help. When they said their names were Mr. and Mrs. Wittmer, they were eagerly invited to come aboard.

As they told the story of what had brought them to Chatham Island, we realized that we were taking part in yet another episode of the strange story of the Floreana colony. We learned that Mrs. Wittmer was again pregnant. In this condition she had been attacked and very seriously injured by a large goat. Nothing could be done for her on Floreana. A week after she was hurt, however, the governor happened to come to the island on an inspection trip. He at once took her in his launch to the hospital at Progreso. Mr. Wittmer accompanied her in case the consequences should be serious, but the children were left behind. The son who had come with the family in 1932 was then about twenty-two, and the baby, who was the first Floreana native, was about eight.

Mrs. Wittmer recovered after some time in the hospital, and the couple made plans to return to Floreana. But although the governor again offered them his launch, there was not enough petrol on the island for them to make the 120-mile trip.

Without hesitation they had come to us in hopes of getting a ride home, for during their nine years on the island they were used to asking passing ships for help. Our itinerary did not include Charles Island, but we did want to help them. In spite of the fact that we had hardly enough petrol for our own journey, Mrs. Mandel gave them one drum each of petrol and oil. She also gave them an assortment of first aid supplies, which are things you simply cannot make on an island, and entertained them at a meal aboard the *Carola*.

While we were with them, we asked many questions about their lives, which they answered with fascinating details about their struggle for existence during nine years. However, we felt we could not ask about the murders for fear of offending them, and they proffered no hint of what they knew. I often wondered what had occurred to make them change their original plan of staying on the island for only four years, as Miss Strauch mentions in her book; perhaps it was the secret of the murders which held them, or simply that they had become used to island life and liked it.

Evidently some people liked living there, as we had discovered earlier in the expedition when we called at Charles Island to pick up the mail at Postoffice Bay. At that time we met Mr. and Mrs. Elmer Conway, an American couple who had come to live there. They were entertained at lunch aboard the *Carola*, where we were all struck by the fact that they seemed perfectly content with their lot. They were very willing to answer all the questions we put to them about their lives: they lived by farming and hunting, and Conway was writing a book. After our lunch the Mandels gave them supplies, and we took them back to Black Beach, from where they would have a reasonably short walk home.

At Black Beach our landing party found a group of Ecuadorian fishermen, who were trying, as the captain did in Dr. Ritter's time, to organize a fishing station here. They infuriated me quite unintentionally by saying, when we asked them if we would find marlin or sailfish in these waters, "Oh, if you want to catch marlin, go to Cuba!"

We met other interesting residents of the Galapagos, including a man from Alsace-Lorraine, who produced a calling card to introduce himself, and an old Icelander with a long white beard. He summed up life on the Galapagos very succinctly by saying, "*Pueblo chico, infierno grande*—little town, big hell!"

12

Restocking an Aquarium

AFTER the Mandel expedition I went directly from Panama to join the fifth George Vanderbilt expedition aboard the *Pioneer*. This took me to a certain extent back to the territory I had covered on the *Carola*. But I will always be fascinated by the Galapagos, for no matter how many times I go there, I am certain to find something new.

When I landed in Florida after the Vanderbilt expedition, it was very nearly time for me to be in Wedgeport to open the tuna fishing season. It wouldn't have mattered if I had been a little late except that I had promised to make a radio broadcast early in July about the season's prospects. My wife and I were faced with a mad dash from Florida to Wedgeport.

We drove day and night up through the southern states to New York, alternately taking the wheel, and even resorting to pills to keep awake. When we got into New Jersey and I realized that we might just miss the steamer which sailed from New York to Yarmouth, I called the shipping officials, told them my story, and asked them to delay the steamer if we had not arrived by sailing time.

But we did arrive, by dint of driving as fast as was legal, just a few minutes before the steamer was due to sail. Once on it, we could relax, for nothing we could do would make it go any faster; also we had to rest up for the next dash from Yarmouth to Halifax. As things turned out, I got to the studio in time for a rehearsal before the broadcast. Within a few days I had boated the first tuna of the season; it weighed 5 hundredweight.

During this season, which was to be the last for many a year

(although we did not then know it), Vanderbilt was busy
making plans for a sixth expedition, which would make as complete a survey as possible of the fish in the Amazon River. The
plans excited me very much, for the Amazon would be completely new to me. After I left Wedgeport, I went back to West
Palm Beach to spend the next few months working out the
details of the trip, which we had planned to begin from Miami
on January 1st, 1942.

Pearl Harbour shattered it all, less than a month before we
were to set out. Vanderbilt turned over the *Pioneer* to the navy
and entered the service himself. Since I was by this time too
old for active duty, I was appointed Chief of Traveller Censor-
ship in Miami. I spent the war cooped up in a building from
which I investigated all ships and aeroplanes that came in or
out of the port. I headed a staff of eleven officers and 150 em-
ployees, but despite the job's importance I found the office
work irksome. My big hands were made for rowing boats,
mending nets and handling fish, not for holding a pen or
hitting typewriter keys.

To get some activity and keep in the fresh air, I spent all my
week-ends and vacations in the Coast Guard Temporary
Reserve, stationed in Miami. I was a chief petty officer—the
highest rank I was allowed to hold without becoming a desk
worker. I instructed younger men and spent considerable time
patrolling the coast. My wife and I moved to Miami during
this time, but although I knew its coast as well as I knew the
Palm Beach area, I could not fish during the war. Neither
could I collect, for aquaria had been emptied and museum
staffs were fighting.

But I still had plans and dreams. Not the least of these had
sprung from a meeting about a year earlier with Fred D. Coppock, a businessman from Greenville, Ohio. Coppock was one
of the first men to see the possibilities of developing southern
Florida, where he had been wintering since 1908. He had
bought much real estate around Miami. He was also very interested in fish; in Ohio, where he owned large gravel-digging
companies, he had begun fish farms in his disused gravel pits.

He wanted very much to see an aquarium in Miami, and we

discussed the project at length. Remembering my aquarium on the Palm Beach Pier, I entertained dreams of another such collection of fish, but on a much larger scale. Coppock had done more than dream: in 1940 he had bought a piece of land on Sunny Isles, just north of Baker's Haulover Inlet. But Pearl Harbour ended this plan too, and Coppock and I could do nothing but talk for the next four years.

In 1945, the plans were revived. But we found that during the war years other people had also been dreaming; both the Dade County Commission and the University of Miami were thinking of building aquaria. Negotiations dragged on through endless meetings, discussions, plans, compromises. Deciding that our dream had bogged down irrevocably, I left Coppock to struggle for it while I earned my living elsewhere. If anything *should* come of it, I would help to design and stock the aquarium, but I was very pessimistic.

Meanwhile Marine Studios at Marineland, farther up the Florida coast near St. Augustine, was reopening after the war. This aquarium, which had been conceived as a great "window" into the sea, a place where people would be able to see fish against a natural background, had originally opened on June 23rd, 1938, and had been tremendously successful. When the war came, the specimens were turned back to their natural home, and the great tanks remained dry for four years. Now that it was time to fill them again and stock them with inhabitants, I was appointed collector of specimens.

Marine Studios consisted of two huge tanks or "oceanaria" which housed great numbers of porpoises, sharks, and reef fish. The aquarium had been the brainchild of Ilya Tolstoy and W. Douglas Burden, who had originally planned it to be used in movie-making and scientific study. They were amazed when it proved to be so popular with the visiting public. It was the largest and most elaborate outdoor aquarium in the world until the Seaquarium was built.

Tolstoy, who was the grandson of the author of *War and Peace*, had done most of the collecting for it himself before the war. In fact he had been interested in wild-life since he was a small child. He had conducted many experiments in the use of anaesthetics to make sharks and other big fish docile when captured. For a while I used his methods for anaesthetizing my captives, but so little was known about the effects of anaesthetics on the systems of fish that the mortality rate was very high. I do not use anaesthetics at all now in my collecting.

To return to my story: the reopening of Marine Studios was scheduled for March, 1946, which left me about six months to restock the two big oceanaria. In that time I collected thousands of fish. Instead of making one long trip I made several short ones because of the necessity of bringing fish to the tanks as quickly as possible. Besides many thousands of small reef fish, I collected a number of jewfish (none under a hundredweight); five sailfish, which died, as nearly all game fish do in captivity; eight barracuda, all at least five feet long; two tarpon, game fish which *will* survive in tanks; about a dozen moray eels, six porpoises, several big sea turtles, three tiger sharks, a sawfish, and a manta weighing a ton.

That manta presented a huge problem to us because at first there seemed no way of transporting it to the tanks once we had brought it to the beach. The collecting boats for Marine Studios numbered three: the *Beau Gregory*, a forty-five-foot cruiser with a live-well; and two skiffs, the *Dolphin* and the *Penguin*. There were also a few live-well barges which could be lashed to the *Beau Gregory*. But although we could use this equipment when we went after the manta, it was not helpful after its capture.

The day we took the manta my two assistants and I were out in the *Dolphin*. Since we had experienced very bad luck with one or two we had previously captured, we needed another, which we were specifically looking for at this time. A few miles out to sea from Marineland we saw a large, dark object moving slowly along the surface about a mile ahead of us. Cautiously we moved towards it until we could see that it was a large manta, cruising along just under the water. When we were close enough, we sent a harpoon dart into the left wing, hoping, as we always did with a manta, to be able to fix a dart in the other wing as soon as possible so we could guide the creature's course.

But this manta was so strong that it towed our skiff out to sea for more than two hours before we could put the other dart in it. All three of us pulled at the line to bring the creature closer, but in doing so we pulled out the first dart, and then, when we had fixed it in again, we pulled out the other one. The darts were pulled out and replaced no less than four times during the next five hours, during which the manta was still towing our boat. At length we were able to control the manta's direction a little and we turned it, much as you would guide a horse by pulling on the reins, towards Marine Studios. We were then six miles out to sea.

But now the manta was at least fleeing in the direction we wanted to go; soon we brought it to the beach. My two assistants swam ashore with the harpoon lines and tied them up at a place from which we could try to bring the manta to the tanks.

Twenty or twenty-five of the Marine Studios staff came down to the beach with a large tarpaulin on which we planned to drag it. But all of us together could not even move the creature. We thought hard about what we could do to bring it in, for after such a struggle it seemed a shame to let it go again. First of all we had to tow it back into deeper water for the night. We tied the harpoon lines securely to stakes on shore and allowed the fish plenty of room to swim.

The next morning we spent a great deal of time constructing a large sled-like platform by nailing together several pieces of two-by-four planks. Then we swam out to float this under the manta. It had completely recovered from its fight the day before and looked very ready to tow us for another seven hours at least. After we had floated the platform under the manta, we attached it to an amphibious "duck"—this vehicle is one of the few good things which came out of the war—and drew the manta up to the beach. We hoisted it by a derrick into the tank, where it soon swam as freely as it had in the sea. It measured eighteen feet from wing tip to wing tip.

Another kind of fish presented a somewhat different towing problem, as three of us discovered one day when we were looking for jewfish. We were in one of our two skiffs, about two hundred miles down the coast from Marineland, not far from

Salerno on the St. Lucie Inlet. This coast was the one I had known since 1909 when I first came to Florida and wintered at Jupiter. It was a very good place for jewfish until the spear fishermen learned about it; when we came to search for them for the Seaquarium, there were none left.

But this was ten years after the day I recall now, when I suddenly felt on my hook something very heavy, heavier and larger than a jewfish. We were using rope half an inch thick, but when the large creature, whatever it was, took my hook, it was all we could do to hang on to the rope and slowly try to bring him up enough so that he would tow our boat. But he would not come up very far. After an hour or so of pulling until our arms threatened to break, we finally hauled him up near the boat. He was a sawfish, at least fifteen feet long, and he was flailing about him with his saw in the most dangerous way.

When I wrote earlier about the broadbill swordfish which got trapped in a lagoon and died before we could bring him to the Seaquarium, I mentioned that swordfish are often confused with sawfish because their names sound alike. But the two fish are very different. A sawfish is a member of the same family as the sharks and rays; it has no bones in its body, but instead a cartilaginous structure. A creature which dwells on the bottom of the sea (which is the reason why ours was so reluctant to come up), the sawfish is the colour of sand on the top and is pale, almost white, on the bottom. It feeds by killing whatever it wants with the double-edged saw it carries on the front of its head. Then it swims across its prey to pick it up in the mouth which is beneath the saw. When you see a sawfish from beneath, it looks as if there are eyes on either side of this mouth, but in fact these are air holes and the eyes are on top of the head.

The saw is sometimes as long as three feet, with teeth of about an inch and a half. Since the baby fish is born with its saw, nature has arranged things so that the saw is covered with a smooth fleshy sheath. Thus it will not hurt the mother during the birth process. This sheath falls off soon after birth.

The sight of a sawfish, although welcome to us because it was a magnificent specimen, brought all kinds of problems to our minds. First of all we had to keep the saw away from the skiff; it could do damage if it started swinging at the sides. Then we had to get a live-well long enough to take the fish 200 miles back to Marineland. The one we had with us was only ten feet long. Finally there was the problem ever-present with a specimen: would it live?

We towed the sawfish, well to the rear of the skiff, to the shore, where we connected the fish with a rope to a sturdy tree. Then we set off to look for some old abandoned boat which could be converted to a live-well barge. Any boat becomes a live-well when you fix it up so that it has water easily flowing in and out and yet floats.

About three miles up the coast near Salerno we found an old motor launch washed up high on the shore by hurricanes. It was twenty-five feet long and perfect for our requirements. The villagers of Salerno, who were glad to be rid of the unsightly hulk, helped us in our work of converting it. This took us two days, for we had to drill holes in the sides to let the water in and out, patch the bottom of the boat and fix empty oildrums all round the inside walls so that it would float. At last we launched it and towed it off to our sawfish.

The fish seemed none the worse for captivity, so it seemed likely it would survive the journey to Marine Studios. We listed the makeshift live-well until the gunwale was well submerged, slid the sawfish in, and righted it. We attached two ropes from the saw to the sides of the barge so that the saw would stay securely in the middle and not tear up the sides. It was not the boat we were worrying about so much as the damage the fish might do to its saw, for this would ruin it as a specimen. The ropes also made the fish lie in a natural and comfortable position for its journey, even though it showed by its fighting that it really didn't want to be comfortable.

We added a few leopard rays and round-ended sting rays to the well, nailed some boards across the top, and in the *Beau Gregory* began to tow the boat back to our base, 200 miles to the north. By this time we had quite a flotilla, for besides the *Beau Gregory* and the improvised live-well we had one of the other boats towing our original live-well, and two skiffs.

Just inside the St. Lucie Inlet there was a swirling tide-rip where the St. Lucie joined the Indian River. We approached this carefully, but as we crossed it, the worst happened: our new live-well turned right over.

Struggling against the tide, we managed to reach the overturned boat in a skiff and run a line round the middle of it. With a grappling hook we grabbed and held the gunwale of the live-well which was nearest the skiff; the skiff towed the live-well broadside, and the *Beau Gregory*, which had been towing the well before it turned over, pulled it ahead. In this manner we were eventually able to turn the well right side up. Then we brought it into quieter waters close to the shore and looked at our cargo. To our amazement, the sawfish was still there, still lashed with its ropes.

But our troubles were not over. The following day something went wrong with the *Beau Gregory*: her shaft log went loose and shook off the outside stuffing box. It seemed as if everything was conspiring against the sawfish and against us; when we reached the nearest shipyard at Melbourne, twenty-eight miles farther up the coast, we found all the ways occupied and no one available to give us any repairs. We had to anchor the live-well and leave it while we went on to the next shipyard, seven miles father north at Eau Gallie. Here at last we were able to get on the ways and have temporary repairs done. We could not wait for a permanent job, since that would take several days and we were still hoping to get the sawfish back in good condition.

We had to return to Melbourne by night and pick up the live-well barge; then, holding our breath against any further mishaps, we continued north. At the end of six more days of cautious progress we arrived at the Marineland basin, where the sawfish was unloaded. Despite all that happened, it was in excellent condition and lived for many a happy day in the oceanarium.

Almost the only game fish which will live in the confinement of an aquarium tank are tarpon and bonefish, and even these it is very difficult to bring in alive. They are small, which is why they will live in captivity, but since they have all the best instincts of game fish, they will not let themselves be taken until they are nearly dead of exhaustion. If they could be caught in a net, they would not have to struggle so, but the only way to bring them in is by playing them as one does a game fish; in this way they are only injured in one place—the mouth—while a net might injure them over their delicate eyes or tear off their scales.

This, then, is where my past as a sports fisherman and my present as a collector come together, as I try to persuade a great tarpon to give up fighting while there is still enough strength left in him to adapt to life in a tank. It is difficult to do this: the furious leaping, high jumping, and shaking a tarpon does in an effort to free itself from the hook are not really natural for a fish. The violent twists of the body tend to severely strain the vertebrae and rupture the internal organs. A land animal which has exerted itself violently to escape capture can lie in hiding until its body recovers from its punishment, but a fish cannot cease to swim. In addition, the tarpon is a fish which must constantly come up to the surface for a breath of air. When it gets very exhausted it cannot come to the surface and consequently drowns.

I did succeed in obtaining two tarpon for Marine Studios, but they were the only survivors of many attempts. Too often the story was what happened when we were trolling for tarpon one afternoon just inside the St. Augustine Inlet. Because we had seen many tarpon in the area, we had anchored the live-well barge close by, aiming to play the fish from one of the skiffs and work them near to the barge for quick transfers to the live-well.

Two of us fished and another steered the boat. Suddenly I got my hook into a large fish, which I began to play. It came out of the water in several very high jumps, and the sun dazzled our eyes as it reflected from its silver sides. A tarpon has very large thick scales, which on a very large fish may be as long as three inches across and which make the fish look as if it were wearing armour.

As we saw it leap up, we judged that the tarpon would measure over six feet. My assistant reeled in his line to give me plenty of room, and the man at the helm manœuvred the boat to follow the fish's flight. We wanted at any cost not to pull too hard on it. I played it very gently, trying merely to tire it and not kill it.

When after half an hour we had gone about a quarter of a mile away from the live-well barge, we began to get anxious about the distance. The fish made several jumps, but then decided to settle down to long runs, sudden turns, and deep soundings. Each time he gave a little line the helmsman would steer as much as possible towards the barge. As the fish tired, he was able to do this more and more, until finally we were alongside, and my assistant and I were able to jump to the barge's gunwales.

I continued to play the fish from the stationary boat, but no matter how I tried to lead him into the live-well while he was still strong, he resisted—bent on his own destruction. Each time I got him near the boat, he would show renewed energy and tear off again. Finally I got him to the gate of the live-well, and he gave up the struggle and swam in.

We were greatly elated when we closed the gate and looked at his silver length. But he began swimming all round the sides of the well, looking for an opening to escape, and then, as though dispirited at not finding one, he stopped swimming and turned over on his side.

We weren't going to give up, though. We picked up the anchor of the barge as quickly as possible and began to tow it back to Marine Studios, sixteen miles down the coast, which we hoped to reach while the fish still lived so that it could be put into the main tank. There it would have room enough to swim and would find itself in a more natural setting.

While we went along as fast as we could, my assistant jumped into the live-well and began to walk the tarpon round, just as we had walked the sharks and the swordfish. To guide it he gripped the fins, which moved only feebly, although the gills were working. The fish seemed to have lost interest in living. Occasionally my assistant would let go of the fins to see if he could swim without help, but each time, after a feeble effort, he fell over on his side.

Throughout the three-hour ride to Marineland we tried everything we knew to revive the fish, for he was a really fine specimen. We even gave him an injection of adrenalin. But he had fought too long and too hard: as we pulled into the dock at Marineland, he gave up and died. All we could do was haul him up on the dock and admit failure.

13

Catching Porpoises

MARINE STUDIOS uses a porpoise as its symbol, and the training originated by the Studios for this highly intelligent mammal is now a specialty there. Crowds gather every day to watch the tricks which the porpoises perform with every sign of understanding perfectly and enjoying thoroughly what they are doing. They leap out of the water as high as twenty feet to take fish from their trainer's hand; they jump through hoops; they play with balls. And when they are not performing for an audience, they can be seen swimming round the tank making up games of their own.

The warm-blooded porpoises are members of the whale family, or to be more exact, they are classified as toothed whales. The kind you see in many large aquaria are correctly called bottle-nosed dolphins—not to be confused with the dolphins which are fish and very much smaller. Bottle-nosed dolphins are blue-grey along their backs, but their underparts are paler, and on some specimens even pink. Their snouts join their heads in such a way that it looks as if they are always smiling, as no doubt they often really are, for porpoises are animals which thoroughly enjoy being alive.

On top of a porpoise's head is a blowhole, exactly as in a whale. In the aquarium you can hear the porpoises regularly coming to the surface and making blowing sounds through this hole as they breathe. They can also make many other sounds through the blowhole—under water they continually speak and chatter to one another—but they have no vocal chords. Trainers have taught them to communicate by opening their mouths and making a rattling sound.

Porpoises have the horizontal tail of the sea mammal and they swim along by waving this tail up and down in a graceful motion. They have a central dorsal fin, a characteristic of many members of the whale family, and two pectoral flukes or fins which look much like arms. Inside their mouths are rows of small teeth, but these are used for gripping, not chewing; the porpoise swallows its food whole. Its eyesight under water is so good that the sight of a visitor can attract its attention through the portholes of the main tank.

The porpoise is not uncommon off the coast of Florida, where it can be seen near the shore in bays and inlets. Because other fish are its food, one of the main problems when a porpoise is caught and put into the aquarium is getting it to eat dead instead of live fish. (We once solved this difficulty by pulling a dead fish through the water on the end of a line so that it would look as if it were alive.) Once a porpoise does begin eating, however, it adapts more readily to life in captivity than almost any other large sea creature.

At Marine Studios it has been possible for scientists to make a complete study of the porpoise's life cycle, for many babies have been born there. Nature shows her usual ingenuity in arranging the birth of a porpoise, which comes out of its mother tail first instead of head first. Since the porpoise is an air-breathing creature, any baby born head first would drown before it was completely free of its mother. But as soon as the baby is born tail first, the mother and any other female porpoises in the tank get under it and push it up to the surface so that it can breathe. Then the baby is ready to swim with the herd, although it is not completely weaned for nearly a year and a half.

Porpoises swim all the time, even sleeping on the move. They will play with anything in their tanks, from dropped pennies to the jet of fresh water which is constantly being supplied. They even carry objects to this jet, let the jet hurl them out into the tank, and swim after them. A penny dropped into the tank once caused endless amusement for one porpoise who picked it up, swam to the surface, threw up the penny and then caught it again as it fell.

Navy researchers have recently concluded that this remark-

At the Seaquarium : the extremely rare threadfish.

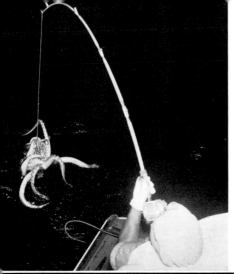

(*left*) Michael Lerner fishing for squid in ghostly garb.

(*below*) Lerner displays giant squid caught off the coast of Peru.

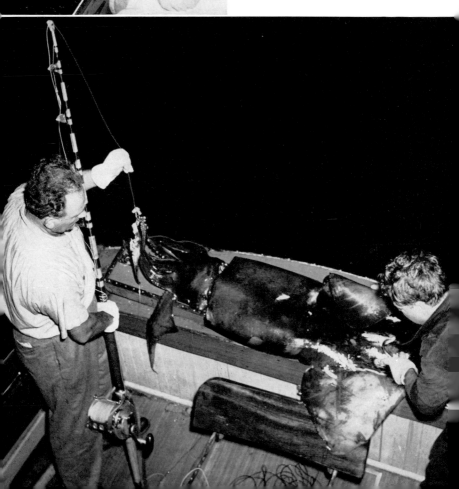

(*Photos: courtesy the Seaquarium*)

(*above*) The pearly nautilus builds a shell for its home.   Like the octopus it crawls on the bottom of the ocean, but it can also move very fast.

(*below*) Male seahorse (left), with pouch for carrying eggs, and female, without pouch.

The unusual sting ray.

A manta ray being hauled ashore to Marine Studios.

Horizontally-striped squirrelfish and long-finned look-downs swim in the Seaquarium's corridor display tank.

(Photo: courtesy the Seaquarium)

The Seaquarium I, launched recently, is the most advanced vessel of its
kind, with a special door in the stern for fish to swim into.

The Seaquarium: foreground, main tank; left, reef tank; rear, filtration plant and circular shark channel; background, maintenance ...ment and landing dock; right, Lost Islands and Seashow Arena.

(Photo: courtesy the Seaquarium)

able animal's brain power equals man's in some aspects, and in some it may even be superior. The porpoise solves difficulties easily, and has the developed sense of maternal responsibility characteristic of animals with a high intelligence. A mother porpoise whose baby has been born dead will spend hours pushing it up to the surface trying to make it breathe. One porpoise in the Marine Studio tanks was given a cathartic hidden in a capsule inside a bluefish; the porpoise ate it, and the medicine did its work, but the porpoise never again ate a bluefish.

Of the special problems involved in capturing porpoises, not the least is just this intelligence. You always have to be one thought ahead. Porpoises will use every opportunity to slip out of the net; they will even co-operate to the extent that one will push down the net and let the others swim over the top of it. When you have finally caught them, however, they are usually ready to admit defeat and make no further fuss. But they have one problem on long journeys in the live-well: they tend to get seasick. This would seem impossible for creatures which spend their lives in the sea, but because the movement of a boat is quite different from the natural motion of swimming, they suffer much as human beings do. As a solution to the problem I devised a sling on deck to put the porpoises in; they can stay out of water for a considerable time with no ill effects. In this sling, the motions of the boat are reduced and the porpoise can travel with not too much discomfort.

The problems of every porpoise hunt are different because of the wily nature of the quarry, but perhaps the strangest hunt I ever went on happened not long after Marine Studios opened. We had just come back from a shark fishing trip in the Studios' collecting boats. Since there was some urgency in the need for two porpoises, however, we decided to try immediately one of the most fruitful porpoise spots we knew—Turtle Mound, about seventy miles south of Marineland on the Intracoastal Waterway and just south of New Smyrna Beach. Instead of going by boat, which would mean a considerable journey, we took a truck loaded with our equipment, just as we did when we were going to pick up a pilot whale. On this occasion we

added an eighteen-foot skiff, an outboard motor, camping
gear, and provisions for a few days of outdoor living, for we
knew what porpoises could be. Early the next morning the
three of us set off down the ocean highway.

At New Smyrna Beach we crossed from the inside of the
Intracoastal Waterway to the long spit of land which forms a
barrier between the waterway and the sea and on which Turtle
Mound is situated. This piece of land is a desolate waste of
sand, mud flats, and mangrove islands, but it has one channel
which we knew from experience was used by the porpoises to
enter a bay on the incoming tide. While the tide was high, they
would gorge themselves on mullet and other fish near the shore
and then they would go out again as the tide ebbed. At the
channel, then, was the best place to trap them, but there
was no place within three miles where we could bring the
truck.

We had to leave it on the last piece of solid ground, and
transport our equipment and camping gear across the bay in
the skiff. It took us three journeys to bring everything. We
then set up our camp well back from the water on the north-
eastern end of the channel, where we were completely hidden
but could easily see the porpoises come in with the tide.

The width of the channel was about eighty yards and it was
about half a mile long, eventually opening into the Intracoastal
Waterway. It was about twelve feet deep, and the bottom had
few rocks or snags. After we had made our camp, our first
operation was the transporting of the huge porpoise net, 100
yards long, across the channel to the opposite side, where it
was then ready to be dragged across to our side to stop the
porpoises' exit once they were in the channel.

When this was done, we hid the skiff in a creek near our
camp and addressed ourselves to the preparation of supper.
Porpoises are alarmed by anything strange in their normal
haunts, and if we had left the skiff in an obvious position, it is
quite likely they would have turned round and gone to seek
another inlet. There were no porpoises nearby when we made
our preparations, and this was lucky, for if there had been, they
would have gone off and mysteriously warned their com-

panions. We expected them in on the midnight tide, but until then we could relax.

We made a fire and indulged ourselves in the delights of fresh fish, for one of my assistants had gone off to catch mullet and the other came back with roasting oysters. Eaten right out of the water like this, seafood is the best possible meal. We sat round the fire after the meal feeling like kings, but we knew we had a full night's work ahead of us.

As darkness fell the mosquitoes came swarming round us from the mangrove swamps, and the sand gnats added their stings to make sure that every bit of uncovered skin was attacked. We put out the fire and decided to try sleeping in the intense heat under blankets to escape the mosquitoes and gnats for the next few hours. Each of us took his turn watching the channel for porpoises for an hour at a time, while the two others pretended to sleep. The man on watch suffered the most intensely from heat because he had to wear boots and oilskins to keep off the insects.

Nothing happened during the first watch, but during the second I was wakened from a semi-sleep by my assistant shaking me and whispering, "They're coming in. Five came through and there may be more."

We got up, put on oilskins and boots, and went as quietly as we could to the edge of the channel, opposite the side where we had left our nets. As with the manatee, we waited not to see the porpoises, but to hear the sound of their breathing through their blowholes. (The noise can be heard for about a hundred yards on a quiet night.) But although we waited for about half an hour, we heard no blowing. That meant there were no more than five porpoises in the bay, but these were enough to give us a margin of error in capturing the two we wanted.

We got the skiff out from its hiding-place, rowed over to the other side of the channel, and pulled the net across. When it was firmly tied at both ends, we loaded a similar net into the skiff and went back again to a point at the opposite side. There we left the net on the bank, intending to wait until the porpoises had finished eating mullet and were making their way back to the sea before we closed it across the channel. Then we would have the porpoises trapped between the two nets.

After about an hour of watching in complete silence, we heard the first blowing noise of a porpoise returning to the sea. Then we heard another, and another, until we counted five. We waited for a few moments, just to give the porpoises time to get well up the channel, and then we reached for the net.

This was a very critical moment, for if the porpoises were to get too far up the channel to the other net, which had already been stretched across, they would turn round and swim back so fast that they would be out at our end before we had a chance to make our blockade. But we did manage to make it—with only seconds to spare: just as we reached the other side and tied the net securely to a tree stump, all five porpoises came streaking down the channel. When they saw they were trapped at this end, too, they inspected the net from one side to the other and went back to try the other end.

Now we could do nothing but wait for the tide to go out again, when it would be easier to handle our captives. So we re-lit the fire, made ourselves another luxurious meal for breakfast, and listened to the porpoises as they swam up and down the channel, snorting and puffing through their blow-holes in protest against being trapped.

Even though porpoises are such very good jumpers, we had found from experience that they do not jump the nets when they have plenty of room to swim, but only resort to a jump when they are penned in very closely. But there were other dangers, not the least of which was, as I have said before, that one porpoise would pull down the net and allow the others to swim out over it. They might also try to smash their way through the net with a head-on charge, become tangled in it, and drown.

As soon as dawn appeared, grey and not very inviting, we began the next stage of the hunt. The family of five porpoises could be seen restlessly swimming from one end of their trap to the other. It was time for the tide to slacken, so we took out a third stretch of net and put it in the skiff.

Our idea was to use this third piece of net to crowd the

porpoises into a much smaller area so that we could eventually beach them. I took one end of the net to the south bank, and one of my assistants took the other end to the farther bank. The third man stayed in the skiff and, instead of rowing, pulled himself along by the cork-line at the top of the net. When we had the porpoises trapped between this sweep net and one of the two stop nets we had originally stretched across, the man in the skiff took the boat to the man on the other bank, who got in with his end of the net; they both brought it over to my side, making a smaller and smaller circle with the intention of eventually pulling the porpoises out on the beach with it.

That was the theory, anyway, but the porpoises had other—and better—ideas. The sweep net was very heavy, and it was a long and slow process for the two of us to pull it along from the banks. All went well, however, until the two men were nearly across the channel in the skiff and the circle was almost completed. Then a large bull porpoise charged at the sweep net, striking it right in the middle with the full force of his heavy body. This caused the top of the net to dip down, and two other porpoises were away before we could stop them. We were not worried by this since we still had three in the net, and in any case the other two were unable to reach the open sea because of the stop nets.

As I stood on shore holding my end of the net, watching the three porpoises circling while the two men came nearer and nearer in the skiff, I was very surprised to feel a sudden tug on the net and a succeeding pull which nearly unbalanced me. I could see the porpoises, and I knew the pull did not come from them, so it must have been something else we had not anticipated. I tried with all my strength to hold my end of the net, but I was definitely being pulled into the water. I had a piece of rope on the end, but I was being drawn away from the tree stumps where I might have tied it. All I could do was try to hold on and yell for help.

The two men in the skiff hastily tied their end of the sweep net to the cork-line of the stop net and came over to me, where I was almost waist-deep in water and quickly losing strength.

The three of us managed to hold the end of the net, but we were not quick enough to prevent the three other porpoises from escaping round it. We were discouraged: at the very least, we would have to go through the whole manœuvre again.

But first we had to get rid of whatever was in the bottom of the net, so we pulled and hauled and heaved and finally brought up a huge manatee or sea cow, at least fifteen feet long and weighing very nearly a ton.

Now what were we to do? We didn't want a manatee, for there were plenty nearer Marine Studios than this. If we released it, it would only get tangled up in the net again. We didn't want to kill it, for apart from knowing that there was a state law against doing so, we felt that such destruction would be wanton and cruel.

Finally we decided to tie the sea cow to a tree and keep it out of our way until we got the porpoises. The manatee resented this very much, not realizing that we were only tying it up for its own good; it splashed heartily with its big flat tail and drenched us all. But finally we got a rope round its tail and tied the rope to a convenient tree, leaving the manatee with its body in about three feet of water so that it could lift its head to breathe.

Weary as we were, we started off again to recapture the porpoises with the sweep net. This time three of them escaped, but we kept telling ourselves we only needed two, and here they were in the net. As we drew the net nearer and nearer, the two porpoises began to look all round for a way to escape. We began to fear they would jump, but instead the bull—it may well have been the same one as we had the first time—charged the net in a mad dash for freedom. He floundered round so much that his pectoral fins got entangled in it; one of the men in the skiff lunged for his tail with a rope.

Of course the other porpoise had slipped out as soon as the top of the net went down, but at least we had one. We pulled it up on to the beach, freed it from the tangles of the net, and tied the tail rope to a tree stump in the same way as we had done with the manatee. We left the porpoise in shallow water with plenty of opportunity to breathe.

We turned back to make another sweep, but we found that the intelligence of the porpoises had told them they would get caught if they stayed together. Now they were scattered at every corner of the trap, and it took a great deal of patience to get two finally within the compass of the sweep net.

We were getting these two in nicely when precisely the same thing happened as before—something got tangled in the bottom of the net—only the net began to pull in the centre, not on the shore end. I went to help, thinking we had another sea cow, but when we finally got our burden in shallow water, it proved to be a lemon shark.

The shark was twelve feet long and, like the manatee, an excellent specimen for an aquarium, but we could not possibly take it back to Marine Studios without a live-well and we had only the truck. Se we put a rope round its tail and tied it to a tree. We now had three captives tied to trees in different parts of the channel!

Of course the lemon shark, which is one of the most vicious of its kind, had pulled at the net enough to allow the porpoises to escape. Because the tide was now rising again, we could not make another sweep. There was nothing to do but check on our small menagerie to see that it was well and eat a large lunch. Waiting for slack tide, we wondered what else we would have to rope to a tree before we could get the porpoises.

Back at the sweep net again, we sighed with relief when we encountered no underwater pull this time. We had all four porpoises in the net and were drawing them nicely towards the shore when they began to get very panicky. Suddenly they all charged the net at the same time and got entangled, as the bull had done. One, more wily than the others, worked itself free and swam over the net. But we managed to drag each of the others into very shallow water to render them helpless for a while.

Which one we should keep was decided on the basis of appearance, for they were all cows (we had a bull tied up). The smartest looking one, with the smoothest skin and the least blemishes, was roped round her tail. We floated the others back into deeper water, where they swam freely as if nothing had happened to them.

Now we had our porpoises; we could strike camp, take up the stop nets, and transport everything back to the truck three miles away. Because it took four separate journeys in the skiff to take back all the gear and the wet nets, it was after dark by the time we returned for the porpoises, which we proposed to transport one at a time.

It was not difficult to load the cow porpoise into the skiff; once there she was tied down so that she would stay in the centre and not capsize the skiff by adding her considerable weight to one side or the other. When we reached the truck, we soaked a mattress with water and with the aid of a fisherman who happened to be passing by, we lifted the porpoise on to the mattress in the back of the truck. We tied her well and covered her with wet blankets so that her skin would not crack. She was quite happy, although she looked a little like an invalid, when we left her and returned for her mate.

As we came across the water, we could hear him breathing angrily through his blowhole even above the noise of the outboard motor. We drew alongside him in the skiff, expecting to be able to lift him aboard, but he was not going to allow us to do this. He was one of the few porpoises I have ever taken which gave us a fight after he was captured; the behaviour of the female was much more typical.

He jerked and jack-knifed his body when we touched him; he lashed his tail; he knocked us down; he went into a rage of splashing and thrashing so that we could accomplish nothing. It was obvious we couldn't lift him aboard simply by taking him and grabbing him.

As always in the collecting profession, we had to think up a new trick. This time we decided to try to roll the porpoise into the skiff, since we could just about push and pull him but not lift him.

We took off the outboard motor and emptied the skiff of everything which was inside it; we got behind it in the water and lifted one side until the skiff filled with water and sank. Then, somehow, getting splashed continually, we managed to roll the porpoise into the middle of the sunken boat and under water we tied him securely between its two sides. Next we tied ropes to the skiff and hauled it up until it grounded, with the gunwales just above water. We bailed out as much water as we could, but naturally a substantial amount was left in the bottom of the boat with the porpoise, who for the moment seemed quiet. We put another rope on him, however, to make sure of him.

In the dark we could not see him very clearly, but we estimated he would weigh nearly 4 hundredweight. We reloaded all the gear and put back the outboard motor, hoping the boat with so much water in it would hold all of us. Because there was some doubt about the matter, we decided on a course which would take us over very shallow water, where we could push if necessary.

Since this was our last trip to the spot, we unroped the manatee and the lemon shark, which very gratefully swam off. Then we departed, precariously.

About half-way to the truck the porpoise lost his temper again and began to twist and turn in the bottom of the boat, shifting his weight from one side to the other so that we shipped even more water. Since luckily we were over a flat, one man and I jumped out, and the other stopped the motor.

For half a mile the two of us waded along towing the skiff while the other bailed out as fast as he could. When at the end of this distance deep water began again, there was nothing we could do but tie the ropes a little tighter around the porpoise, start the motor, board the boat, and just trust to luck that the porpoise would be sensible about his situation—and ours. The last half mile to the truck was one of the longest I have ever travelled.

By a miracle of luck, we made it. We were more than relieved to see our fisherman friend at the beach to help us. All four of us pulled the skiff as high up on the shore as we could with the aid of a wooden roller. This high position, we felt, might be of use to us if the porpoise decided to make a dash for the water.

As soon as we released the ropes from him, and while he was still in the skiff, the porpoise went into a furious rage. His thrashings knocked us all down; the powerful strokes of his tail broke both thwarts and smashed three planks in the skiff before he rolled out on the ground.

Then it was all we could do to stop him from getting back to the water. We certainly could not move him up the bank, for it took the strength of all four of us to simply hold him where he was. At last he quieted down, probably from exhaustion.

We had with us a large sling made of canvas attached to two pipes for handles; we managed to roll the porpoise on to this and to lift him on to the mattress on the back of the truck, next to his lady friend, who had no doubt admired his show of resistance to capture. But at last he seemed to be subdued. We roped him securely and covered him with more wet blankets. He was bruised, cut and bleeding; so were we, and we had a broken boat as well.

We had no more trouble on the way home and pulled into Marine Studios just as dawn was breaking for the second time since we had left. While we watched those two porpoises being put into a special tank to get acclimatized to their surroundings, I am sure I could see a look in the bull's little eye which said, "I'll get you for this." But before long he had forgotten thoughts of revenge in the enjoyment of his new surroundings.

14

A Short Guide to Collecting

As all my adventures with porpoises have shown, these creatures constantly tax the collector's ingenuity. No exception is the spotted porpoise, a relation of the bottle-nosed dolphin. This spotted creature, which is a deep-sea dweller, is the kind of porpoise usually seen from ships at sea; it is attracted by any moving craft, and will often come racing for over a mile to meet it. Groups of porpoises, which seem to have no difficulty in keeping up with the ship's speed for long distances, often come close enough to be touched by a pole from the rails. But if the speed of the ship is changed, or it goes off in a different direction, the porpoises will immediately leave it and will not return. Perhaps another school will meet the ship later on, but the same one will not.

The spotted porpoise looks not unlike the bottle-nosed dolphin, except that its nose is longer, and large spots appear on it in its maturity. It feeds on what are called pelagic fish (those which live near the surface of the sea) and on squid, and its speed in chasing its prey is supposed to be the fastest in the entire porpoise family.

For a long time we were puzzled about catching these fast swimmers. They don't come into shallow water, so nets are not feasible; they cannot be persuaded to take a baited hook, since they are far too intelligent to let themselves be caught like that; and they cannot be harpooned as you can harpoon a ray, for even if you strike a porpoise in a non-vital part of its body, it will die in a few days from loss of blood and body liquids. We thought it best to try and catch a porpoise by its tail, but how? No porpoise is going to stand still long enough for you to come up behind it and allow you to slip the rope on. We obviously had to have some kind of mechanical device which would slip the rope around the tail from a distance, but yet with complete effectiveness.

We put our heads together and consulted with the engineers at Marine Studios. After many experiments we came up with a tail-grabber which did the job. This consisted of a long pole with a contraption like giant ice tongs at the end. A removable socket was fitted to the end of each arm of the "tongs". A rope running along the pole went through an open eye on one socket and across the span of the tongs; it was spliced securely to the other socket. Thus the part of the rope held by the sockets formed a sliding loop. At the tong-end of the pole was a spring device to hold the whole gadget open until it hit a porpoise's tail.

To use this I stood on the boat and watched until a porpoise came close enough for me to thrust at it, striking it so hard that the impact dislodged a bar keeping the spring open, and the tail-grabber snapped shut. The sockets locked together, and the loop tightened round the hard rubbery keels on the base of the porpoise's tail flukes. The bulky tongs, attached to a separate rope, were shaken free and quickly hauled aboard, and the porpoise remained hung by the tail.

This contraption worked so well that numerous copies were made. They have become standard collecting equipment—part of the gear at the Seaquarium as well as at Marine Studios.

On one occasion two assistants and I went out with a tail-grabber in our skiff the *Dolphin*, in which we headed north from Marineland. We sighted a school or "pod" of porpoises about twelve miles off shore and calculated that if we ran near them, we could expect them to come and accompany our boat, as is their habit. After a few minutes they did in fact take up a position directly ahead and just under our bow. One of my assistants stood ready in the bow with the tail-grabber, another made ready the line, and I handled the boat.

Very skilfully my assistant waited until one large porpoise surfaced; then he lunged with the tail-grabber. The jaws snapped shut, the rope was around the tail, and the metal part, which came swinging loose, was hastily pulled aboard by the other man.

Then the first man began to play the porpoise—which was naturally furious at being caught—much as you would play a large game fish. He let it have all the rope it wanted at first, and then we manœuvred the boat round to follow it, allowing it to pull us along in the first mad rush of its speed. After watching a spectacular display of jumps, runs, and sudden turns worthy of a sailfish, we began to pull the porpoise in because we feared that it might try to escape by sounding so deep that it would drown itself. It took the strength of three of us for half an hour to pull the fighting animal close to the boat. Then we put under it a canvas sling of the same type as we used for the porpoise at Turtle Mound and hauled it into the skiff. This porpoise displayed so much fight that we were thoroughly drenched and the boat thoroughly rocked before we got it in.

We placed it carefully on wet blankets on the stern sheets and securely tied down its $2\frac{1}{4}$ hundredweight of flesh. When we had brought it into Marine Studios, we went out for another. Later we had the satisfaction of seeing both swimming freely in the tank, unblemished by the tail-grabber.

Porpoises can stand quite a lot of handling, provided that they eventually do get to an aquarium and can swim at large to recover from their experiences. A number of them have even been sent by air from Florida to California; bedded down on wet mattresses and covered in soaked blankets, they arrived in very good condition. On another occasion two or three were taken to Bimini by boat from Miami, and they suffered from nothing but slight seasickness. Keeping porpoises damp while travelling is the main requirement; on the flight to California a man sat beside the porpoises all the way, bathing their heads to keep them from drying.

While I was out chasing these porpoises, Coppock was still in Miami working on our dream of a large aquarium there. He, at least, had not been discouraged, in spite of the long-drawn-out negotiations which seemed to go on for years between the Dade County Commission (Miami is in Dade County), the University of Miami, and Coppock's interests.

Finally, after article upon article had appeared in the local papers, and meetings had been held over and over again, Dade County decided to put the issue to a public vote. It wanted to float a bond issue to raise the necessary money, but the public turned it down, not only at one referendum, but again and again.

The University of Miami, which thought an aquarium would enormously help its Marine Laboratory and would greatly benefit public education, also tried unsuccessfully to raise money.

Coppock felt this was his opportunity, and he asked me to help him get the aquarium going. In 1948 I resigned my job at Marine Studios and went back to Miami.

But we had no smoother sailing than the other groups in the planning of our aquarium. There was the difficulty of raising enough money, of finding a suitable site, of designing the buildings, and of working out the details of pumping. These matters were to take another five or six years to iron out, and since they were not in my province, I left Coppock on dry land to use his brilliance at dealing with these things while I took to the water again as a collector on a free-lance basis. I did sit in on the meetings with the men who were planning the aquarium and tried to help with my knowledge of fish and their habits, but financial and legal problems were not my forte.

However, I knew that if and when the aquarium—which was then nameless—were built, it would be my job to stock it. So for my own use during these years and with an eye to the coming aquarium, I had the *Sea Cow*, the *Sea Horse* and the other two skiffs built to my own design. I knew from my experience at Marine Studios that a large live-well was needed and I therefore thought it best to make a barge as large as the boat. The *Sea Cow* was big enough to take a fish twenty feet long and to hold over four thousand gallons of water.

As I have said, a live-well is any boat which will float with water inside it. The idea of it, incidentally, was adapted from fishing boats in the Bahamas, Cuba and Panama; because the natives used to be without refrigeration on their fishing boats, and because on the longer trips from port it was inadvisable to bring the fish in dead, they used live-wells in the middle of their boats to keep the fish alive and fresh until they got to port. If any did die on the way in, they salted or dried the carcasses, but there was a much higher market value on fresh fish.

During my free-lance period I also got together a great deal of other collecting equipment which I knew would be necessary for an aquarium as large as the one we had in mind. Special gear would be needed since commercial fishing equipment is on the whole useless for collecting: if you just put down a net and pulled it up, as commercial outfits do, you would certainly have many fish, but they would tend to be all of one kind. You would also find that numbers of them had damaged eyes or gashes in the flesh from rubbing against the net, and all of them would have lost scales as a result of being pushed against each other. If fish which are damaged in any way are put into an aquarium, they very easily become infected with diseases, particularly tail rot. It is possible to cure them, usually by putting them in a tank full of very weak chemical solution, but their perfection as specimens is gone.

If a net is used for collecting, it is usually a dip net for handling individual specimens; a trawl net for getting fish from the bottom of the sea, where they are largely protected by sponges and seaweed from damage as they come up; or a cast net. This last is usually employed only for collecting bait with which to catch larger fish like sharks, and on one occasion, of which I shall tell later, I used it for catching a shark itself.

The dip net is mostly used in reef and shallow water fishing. By day we go down to the reefs with Aqua Lungs, but at night we light a lamp under water or at the prow of a boat. Since many fish have nocturnal eyes and some eat only at night, before long we find the lamp surrounded by curious fish and crustaceans, just as at night you find a lamp in a room surrounded by moths. Because the light blinds the fish, they are bewildered and do not resist when we lift them out in a dip net. Thus we avoid hurting them.

We fish for other reef fish, like the silvery look-downs, with bait and hook at night. We often take these near bridges, since a stanchion is a very good substitute for a reef. The small hooks do not hurt the fish much.

For vegetarians like parrotfish, which also like bridges and walls, I have specially designed a trap into which we put cabbage, lettuce, or other succulent bait. This trap is fundamentally a large cube made of wire netting, but one of the sides has a large funnel-shaped depression which is pushed into the cube so that it nearly touches the opposite side. When a parrotfish comes through the funnel and starts nibbling the cabbage, he is surprised to find that he can't get out again, because he can't find the entrance, and if he could find it, he wouldn't be able to manœuvre himself round the edge of the funnel to escape. So he is not released until I take up the trap and gently lift him out of it into the live-well.

Since parrotfish, look-downs, and certain other fish live in the same places, I would usually plan to get them on one trip. I would put down my traps for parrotfish in the evening, and then sleep until about one o'clock. In the darkness I would fish for look-downs, which come out at night to feed until dawn. After perhaps an hour more of sleep I would pick up the traps for parrotfish. This could go on for a number of nights.

Collecting is not a job which lets you count on free evenings, or even regularly scheduled overtime. It is often necessary to fish for much longer than you had anticipated. I have often spent whole weeks on the Bimini reefs, completely alone, fishing sometimes at night and sometimes during the day, to fill the live-wells, or to find one particular fish I had orders for.

Off Bimini is the sunken wreck of a concrete ship which Henry Ford thought would greatly help the American Navy to win World War I. Two of these ships were built as an experiment. The trouble with them, however, was not that they wouldn't float, but that concrete is a material which does not give, as do steel and wood, against the stresses and strains of the sea. One of these colossal ships was acquired by a group of liquor dealers and towed to a spot five miles south-east of Bimini, where it was grounded. Here it was converted into a huge warehouse to serve as a supply depot for the convenience of rum-runners during Prohibition. Bootleggers tied their boats alongside by the hundreds and bought whisky, rum, and gin to smuggle into the United States. Naturally the end of Prohibition left this great concrete hull useless. During World War II, however, it was used as a target for bombing practice.

The concrete ship is now a fine artificial reef for fish, and it is one of my favourite collecting haunts. When I want a particular specimen, I use a glass-bottomed bucket, one of the most vital pieces of equipment I have, to look beneath the surface as I float over or round the ship in a skiff. Then I don an Aqualung and step down over the wreck to chase my fish. The water is so clear and blue that the iron skeleton and concrete blocks of the ships can be clearly seen all the way down.

When I am collecting fish from the bottom of the sea, rather than from a real or artificial reef near the surface, my methods, of course, are different. Take sea horses, for example, which are one of the most popular of the smaller fish in an aquarium. It is easy to see why: they look like some illustration to a child's fairy tale as they float upright through the water, their little horse-like heads daintily held erect and their tails curling beneath them. When they come to rest, they wind their tails round a convenient piece of weed for an anchor.

Their construction is curious, for they carry their skeletons not inside their bodies as most vertebrates do, but outside, in the form of bony plates. This accounts for the ridge-like formation of their exteriors. They are relations of the pipefish, and like them have round snouts for sucking in tiny organisms as food. The bony structure round their eyes gives them permanently worried expressions.

Perhaps their most characteristic distinction is that the male incubates the eggs. The female deposits the eggs with an ovipositor, a long pipe-like tube, in the stomach of the male, where he keeps them, even gaining weight in an apparent pregnancy, until they are ready to face life on their own. They then emerge from the male's stomach pouch by an opening just under the neck—often hundreds of them at a single birth.

Since sea horses are found on the bottom of the sea, where

there is plenty of weed, to collect them I use the deep trawl. It is surprising how near to the shore these exotic creatures live: sea horses can be found abundantly in the bay just off Virginia Key in Miami. We go after them with our largest boat, and in the live-well, where we intend to keep them, we put some branches or twigs so that they will feel more at home with something to hitch their tails to.

Then we let out the trawl net, which is funnel-shaped, a long way behind the boat. It has a line of lead along the bottom so that it will sink straight down, and a "skirt", or extra piece of net, to protect the end of the funnel, which is securely tied. When it has been dragging along the bottom for about an hour, we pull it back to the boat by means of a winch and ropes from the hoist. As the bottom of the net comes up, it gets very heavy, for reasons which are apparent when we untie the end. On to the deck pours a shapeless mass of sponge and weed, with fish of every kind: sea horses are entangled in the weed, spiny lobsters crawl out of it, a crab waves its claws; we watch out for scorpionfish, in case we should put our hands on one accidentally and get a nasty sting. The smell from the sponges, grey-green squashy masses, is slightly sickening. The fish splash with their tails and fins, trying to escape; as we stand over the catch, we are liable to get splashed from head to foot with dirty sea water, which eventually dries in the sun to a mass of whitish spots all over the skin.

We unwind the sea horses from their weed and drop them into the live-well. We throw back as quickly as we can filefish, snappers, grunts and crabs, of which we usually have such a plentiful supply that we do not want more. Then we lift out parrotfish, angelfish, flounders, and others which we do want to keep.

Among these are the cowfish, a member of the trunkfish family which has a hard box-like structure covering all its body except the tail. The cowfish is distinguished by the two little horns above its eyes and by the brilliant blue-white of its underside. Few things could be whiter than a cowfish's flat stomach. We also want to keep the frogfish, a creature which, like the scorpion, has a multitude of fins and waving spines;

the frogfish, however, boasts a soft protuberance at the top of its head with a number of waving tentacles on it. This it uses to attract other fish to its vicinity in order to get itself a meal. We also look for the lizardfish, a long slender fish which likes a sandy bottom over which it can slide quickly in a darting motion. We pick out the spiny boxfish, a bigger, longer relative of the pufferfish and a creature which, if disturbed, will swell up and stiffen its spines. Also we are happy to find triggerfish, which have such lovely colours.

Once we have found all the fish we need, we throw back all the weed and sponge and dirty water, wash down the deck, and wash ourselves as well. Then we're ready to begin all over again, sometimes five or six times in one day, until we have perhaps over a thousand fish in our various live-wells.

During this free-lancing period I would often go out to get specific fish ordered by clients and museums in other parts of the country. I supplied many specimens to scientific institutions for experimental purposes, and sometimes I even took scientists collecting with me. One of the many eminent biologists and ichthyologists I met in this way was Dr. Werner Bergmann of Yale University, who was doing research into the way sponges grow.

We took two trips to collect sponges in the Florida Keys; on one of these trips, in 1954, we collected a total of 5,000 sponges in three weeks. We would spend the day bringing them up in nets; in the evening Dr. Bergmann would slice them up as thin as pancakes and leave them to dry overnight on the beach. We had to anchor the boat downwind of them in order to breathe, since the only things which smell worse than a decaying sponge are two decaying sponges! At the end of the trip we crated the sponges and sent them to Yale. A few months later Dr. Bergmann wrote to me and told me that I would not recognize the piles of sponges now: all that was left of them was contained in three one-ounce vials of liquid!

Another interesting excursion during this period of collecting fish on order took place one day about twenty miles south of Miami. I was with an assistant in the *Sea Horse* off a reef on the sheltered side of one of the Ragged Keys. Since it was a dark night, we took to our skiff and put a light in the prow. As we manœuvred over the reefs, we used a pole to push the skiff along, not wishing to frighten our quarry away with a motor. When we came round the outside of the reef to where the water was shallow, we jumped over the side and pushed the skiff instead of poling it along.

Shortly afterwards my assistant saw an octopus in the glare of the lamp. It was undulating along in its characteristic way, using all its eight legs with their round suckers. It seemed to measure about three feet from the end of a tentacle to the end of the one opposite, an ideal size for our needs, for we had an order for just such an octopus to appear on a television show. I often get telephone calls asking me to deliver a live creature, usually a spectacular one like an octopus or a shark, in a studio by a specific time. Somehow it is always managed, although on occasion the creature has been brought to the studio while the first announcements of the programme are being made!

An octopus, like a surprisingly large number of sea creatures, can change colour according to its background, and this one went into a virtuoso performance as the light caught him, even changing separate parts of his tentacles to different colours in an attempt to blend with his background. Since the octopus, having no spines or bones, is regarded as a tasty meal by many fish, this camouflage is the only protection it has.

Capturing an octopus is not simply a matter of scooping it up and putting it in a live-well. Its suckers cling so tightly to the rocks on which it is crawling that if you were to pull, you would break off its tentacles and still not get all the octopus. On this occasion my assistant and I were both in the water, one on either side of the octopus, teasing it gently by poking it with sticks. It was so irritated by this that it kept lifting one tentacle and then another, until finally it shot away from the reef in a kind of jet-propelled motion, pouring out a stream of dark liquid as a smoke screen, just like its cousin the squid.

As it tore away, my assistant scooped it up in the dip net, and we put it in the skiff. But we didn't just put in it a live-well, for we had known octopi before: they can escape from anything, even with the lid down, by sliding their tentacles round corners and under covers. We put the octopus in a plastic bag, making sure it had enough water and air, and tied the top in a knot. Then we stowed it safely to one side of the skiff. There was our television actor, in the bag.

We continued along the reef, seeing what other creatures we could find with our light. Spiny urchins, which look like dark pincushions, sat immobile on the reefs; spiny lobsters, or crawfish, stirred their tentacles from under it; a scorpionfish, which we captured, was lying dangerously on the bottom; barracudas glided by; moray eels looked out from the crevices of the reef to see what the light was. The light reflected from their eyes, which looked like bright jewels under the water.

A little farther along my assistant suddenly told me to stop, for there was a commotion. At the edge of the circle of our light a school of houndfish, blinded and panicked by the glare, were leaping in every direction. Houndfish are a kind of needlefish, the smallest variety of which you can see simply by looking over any bridge in southern Florida. They are slim and green, look exactly like long needles, and have extended beak-like snouts with sharp ends.

These houndfish, however, attain a length of five feet. Their snouts are not only sharp but exceedingly strong and capable of piercing both boats and fishermen. The fish are known for a jump which resembles the throwing of a spear—and it has about as much force.

The school we spotted had settled down for the night over the reef, but now they were very disturbed. They were clearing the water for distances of twenty-five feet, keeping up these jumps for as much as 100 yards, only touching the water with their tails to gather more momentum for another leap. The air seemed to be full of their silver shapes whizzing past like bullets. I felt it was best to escape, for we could catch no more specimens now that everything round us was thoroughly upset.

As I was climbing back into the skiff to get away, a particularly large houndfish, about four and a half feet long, came sailing through the air in great leaps just at the edge of the light. Suddenly it changed course, and before I could move, it struck me like a spear.

Its snout went through my upper calf just under the knee and out the other side, then embedded itself in the wooden planking of the boat. For a moment or two I was pinned there, in such agony that I was hardly conscious, but then the fish tore itself loose and was off again. It probably had not even hurt its snout much.

I collapsed into the skiff and watched the blood ooze, then gush, from the two sides of the wound. This loss of blood probably saved me from worse things, for its flow kept the wound clean. My assistant took me back to the main boat, where he gave me first aid and treated me for shock. After a sleepless night, we managed to get to a doctor, who stitched up my leg. In three weeks I was back on the job.

15

Some of the Hazards

FISH with spears are not the only dangers we collectors can run into. The weather is as great a threat to us as it is to all other fishermen and sailors. In September, 1948, a hurricane hit Florida and caught me in a very vulnerable position.

Craig Phillips, who was later to become curator at the Miami Seaquarium, was my assistant at that time; he and I had been out for a few days on the reefs near Tavernier, which is among the Florida Keys. We had the live-well nearly full of the specimens we wanted, but there were still eight traps set at the bottom of the reefs. It remained only for us to lift these traps on the next day, and then we could go home.

We cooked a good supper to celebrate our last evening at sea and then turned on the radio. We had been so absorbed in our job that we had not even bothered to do this for the past few hours. To our surprise the announcer began to talk about a hurricane. He said that it was gaining momentum and would strike the Florida coast in the Miami area within the next twenty-four hours.

This was all the more a shock to us because the water in our vicinity had been calm and clear and the sky blue all day, with a light breeze just taking off the heat. We looked at each other and wondered what to do. Then we noticed that outside the wind was picking up speed, and the boat was rocking more than it had. Perhaps the hurricane was going to hit us first.

Considering our cargo of specimens and the eight traps, which are not cheap pieces of equipment, in the water outside, we decided that the best thing to do would be to try to pick up the traps in a hurry and then head for Miami as fast as we could. The nearest cut through the Keys to the inside was forty miles north at Angelfish Creek; we might just make it to Miami before the hurricane struck us.

But it didn't look as if we had much chance when we stepped outside and saw the sea getting more choppy. It was growing dark by then; from the skiff it became more and more difficult to see our traps marked with cork buoys. As the sea became rougher and the skiff jogged up and down, to pick them up soon became an impossibility. We were forced to leave four of them and take the others to the *Sea Horse*. We then took up our anchor in a hurry and set our course for Angelfish Creek.

The wind came out of the north-east and got stronger and stronger. Since we were heading north, we had to drive directly into it. Within two hours the wind had reached gale force, and we were making only four miles an hour. The waves hit our prow and crashed right over the cabin. As we heard the water sloshing back and forth in the live-well, we thought about our specimens, but could do nothing.

We set a compass course, since it was too dark and there was too much water continually pouring over the boat for us to see where we were going. We knew that to our left was a dangerous chain of reefs. It was necessary to hold the wheel so firmly to keep the compass point that we had to take it in turns because it was too tiring for only one man. And then the engine began to sputter; we feared it was going to die out, which would be disastrous.

Fortunately, I reasoned that the trouble was probably a clogged petrol strainer, for the petrol tanks were being shaken so violently that the sediment was working through the line. I managed to clean both the petrol strainer and the carburettor. To my relief the engine sounded as healthy as ever when I put them back.

Throughout the night we struggled on, unable—because it was too rough to light a stove—to make ourselves the hot coffee which would have kept our spirits up. So we ate cold food and watched for the dawn. Everything was soaked with sea water inside as well as outside the cabin.

When eventually the grey light began to show in the east, Phillips climbed with great daring to the roof of the cabin to see where we were; he had to crawl on his stomach and hold on to the rail. When he got down again, he said he thought he saw a beacon about a quarter of a mile off. When we reached it a little later, we were delighted to find that the light was at the entrance to Angelfish Creek. Throughout the night, then, we had been steering in the right direction.

As we turned into Angelfish Creek, we felt that our troubles were over. We managed to light the stove and make hot coffee and congratulated ourselves upon our escape. Since our drenched radio as well as everything else was useless, we had no way of knowing that we were far from out of danger.

Winding our way through the length of Angelfish Creek into Biscayne Bay, we imagined the comfort of being at home and in dry clothes. It wouldn't be long now, we thought.

But when we came into Biscayne Bay, the hurricane hit us with all its force. We could not use the shelter of the shoreline, for the water was too shallow for the *Sea Horse*, which drew considerable depth. We had to use the ships' channel about a mile off shore. There we got the full force of the storm: the water crashed continually over the cabin, the wind struck so violently that occasionally the engine was useless against it, and the rain beat down fiercely. Even though it was daylight, we had to revert to a compass course.

I thought once or twice about the specimens in the live-well, but I saved most of my sympathy for myself; water was their natural element, not mine. The one consolation we had was the thought that we were the only boat attempting navigation in such a storm, so there was no fear of collision. All we had to worry about was running aground on a sandbank.

After an hour or so of this, I decided that it was foolish to try to get to Miami in such a storm and that it would be best to ride it out in the safety of a protected basin on an island I knew about twenty miles south of Miami. We changed course and wallowed along, but progress was so slow—we cannot have covered twenty-five miles in the whole of that day—that it was getting dark by the time we were within a mile of the haven.

We realized that in the dark we would never be able to navigate into the narrow channel leading into the basin—if indeed we could ever find it. For the night I decided to work in slowly over the flats and anchor close to the shore. We could only get there because the storm had brought a tide of four or five feet with it, one of its only blessings. We dropped an anchor, but it did not hold, and we drifted off. We managed to run back and drop the anchor again; to make sure, we dropped a second one. It seemed to be safe enough to shut off the motor.

By this time we had been fighting the storm for twenty-four hours without proper food or sleep. Phillips collapsed in sheer exhaustion, and although I tried to stand watch I fell asleep sitting on the warm engine box. When I woke up, I was curled neatly on top of it, and it was nearly dawn.

The anchors had held, but far from abating, the storm seemed to be increasing. We ate scrambled eggs for breakfast, but those eggs needed no breaking or stirring with a fork. Then we tried to start the motor, thinking we saw ahead the island we were aiming for and hoping to make a run for it.

But the water had got into the engine, and nothing would make it start. This seemed like the end to us. Then we heard an aeroplane overhead, and rushing out we saw a Coast Guard plane circling above us. It dived past us and dropped something in the water as it went by. Fishing it out with a net, we found it was a square of balsa wood with a hole bored into the middle. A message, which had been stuffed into the hole with a plug placed over it, warned us to seek shelter, as a hurricane of severe intensity was due to strike in the area in the next few hours.

We read this over and over again, convinced that we had already been through the hurricane, but obviously there was more to come. What could we do? The engine was dead, and the plane which had dropped this horrifying message had already disappeared on its way back to Miami.

As a situation of crisis develops and deepens in intensity, the things which must be saved get fewer and fewer. At first we had been concerned to save the traps; then we had thought about the specimens; now it was obvious that the only essential thing was to save ourselves. Since we had a skiff and an outboard motor in the cockpit, I took both out and decided to try to get help on the island. I stowed an extra five-gallon tank of petrol in the skiff and put on nothing but swimming shorts, for it was useless trying to keep dry. Luckily the outboard started after a few pulls, and I went off, steering with one hand and bailing with the other as the boat tossed among the huge waves. Phillips remained behind, ready to try to reach the shore if I should not get back to the boat.

In the basin, when I finally got there, I found one small boat in very poor condition. I had an inkling who it belonged to, but I wasn't sure until I pulled alongside, and a dark head came up. "My Gawd, man, where you come from?" said a familiar voice. It was Old Joe, a Negro whom everyone in the Keys knew well, and who had been left on the island when others had sought shelter because he did not have enough petrol for his boat.

Since I had five gallons of petrol, I persuaded Old Joe to give me a tow into the basin in exchange for them. We went back together in his old boat, put the anchors from the *Sea Horse* into it, and slowly pulled her into the basin. It was a very difficult and long-drawn-out operation, but we had the strength of desperation by this time.

In the basin we tied every line we could find from the boat to a tree stump or tree trunk along the shore. Then the three of us sat in the cabin while the fury of the storm broke over us. I think the eye of the storm must have been right above our heads, for everything around us was being torn up and thrown in all directions. The palm trees on the shore were laid flat, and in the cabin things hurtled across the room as the boat rocked and strained at the ropes.

I don't know for how many hours we sat, managing to get up and brew coffee whenever the boat was steady enough. Eventually the storm slackened, and the rain stopped beating so hard. The storm had obviously passed over, and we now had just the edge of it to deal with.

As soon as it was calm enough, we lighted two double-burner paraffin lamps, as well as our now usable oil stove, and put them in the cabin to dry out the damp wiring. We looked round for something to eat, but there was hardly anything left. So, repugnant as it was to me, we took some of the specimens out of the live-well and cooked them. Only about twenty per cent of them were still alive, for even a fish cannot stand being buffeted as much as the boat had been during the past two days.

While we were eating, the Coast Guard plane circled overhead and "buzzed" us three times. We waved to it, and when the crew was satisfied that we were all safe, it took off for Miami. Our families had notified the Coast Guard of our plight, and the plane had been sent out to look for us.

We sat and waited throughout the rest of the storm; in the afternoon we cautiously tried the engine again. It started, to our relief, enabling us to set off for home, with Old Joe, whose tired boat had saved our lives, in tow behind. In three hours we were at the dock in Miami, where our families and friends were waiting anxiously. I am afraid that our desire to be home and completely dry made us forget entirely—for once!—the specimens in the live-well.

On another occasion Phillips and I actually lost our boat. We took an expedition full of all kinds of foolishness, which began with my trying to use a cast net to catch sharks. Outside a reef in very shallow water off the Florida Keys we were looking for the small fish which live in such places. Phillips was at the outboard motor; I was standing on the bow with the cast net held in my hands and teeth—as is the correct way with this net—ready to throw it out whenever we saw anything interesting.

A cast net is made of a circular mesh weave and it has a lead line attached to it. When you throw it out, the lead weight sinks rapidly to the bottom, and fish swim into it. Then you pull on the tuck ropes which are attached to the main line and bring up your fish. This mesh bag is a sort of fisherman's lasso, ideal for catching mullet for bait.

As we were cruising along, we came upon two nurse sharks basking in the shallow water. Instead of leaving them alone, as would have been sensible, since we did not have equipment for dealing with sharks, we decided just to see if we could catch them. We chased them along for some time, as I perched with my net.

They stopped after a while, and I let fly with a cast which was better than my average ones, neatly encircling a shark. I pulled the tuck ropes, and my shark was caught. But I hadn't been as smart as I thought, for the handline had tangled round my wrist as I pulled it in; before I could do anything about it, I was in the water on top of the shark.

Phillips at once sprang to help me get free from the rope and the net, but he leaped in the water so quickly that he forgot to turn the engine off. When he freed me from the net and we stood up on a reef to look for the boat, it was rapidly moving away from us. There we were, three miles from the shore, holding a net with a furious shark in it while our boat chugged along merrily 100 yards away!

Luckily outboard motors are made to go in circles when there is no one holding them. Our only fear was that the petrol supply would run out. But the skiff went round in such large circles that eventually it came near the reef, and after several abortive attempts we managed to retrieve it. One of us held the shark while the other swam a short way off the reef and intercepted the boat. Then we brought the shark aboard and took it to the main boat for transport homeward. It appeared none the worse for its long sojourn in the net. As for us, we were helpless with laughter at ourselves.

We were lucky in our encounter with this netted shark— much luckier, I often say, than other people have been with Florida sharks. Because of my frequent expeditions to bring sharks back alive and biting, people often ask me if I think sharks bite people. My only answer to this is, "Do dogs bite people?" I think sharks are dangerously unpredictable: they will bite as unexpectedly as a dog. I don't advise people to bathe where the sharks are known to be abundant and I particularly warn them to keep out of the water if they have any cuts or wounds because sharks get panicky at the smell of blood.

Size is no indication of how dangerous a shark can be. The whale shark—the biggest fish in the world—is totally harmless, whereas a four-foot lemon or tiger shark can become vicious. An old Negro in the Florida Keys used to say: "The onliest sharks I trusts is a dai-ad one." This is a sentiment I share.

When I was in the South Pacific with George Vanderbilt, I heard a terrible story about a native of one of the South Sea Islands who was fishing with a hand-line from a boat. He let his hand trail below the water, and suddenly a shark about four feet long came up and with one slash of his teeth took off the fisherman's hand. Other victims I heard of—and saw— included a young woman who lost a foot while swimming in a lagoon when a shark came up unnoticed, and a pearl diver who lost his arm while diving for oysters. I saw one man who carried on his face the imprint of a shark's teeth; a small shark had darted at his head while he was fishing and slashed at his cheek.

It is this kind of unpredictable attack by a shark which is most to be feared. Two commercial fishermen I know were netting for Spanish mackerel just off Jupiter, my old winter fishing grounds, when they experienced just such an attack. They were hauling in their net, full of mackerel, and watching the usual school of sharks which follow the mackerel. These sharks are of many kinds, but all hope to get a free meal from the nets. On this occasion a large tiger shark, nearly twenty feet in length, was especially persistent; he came right into the net and stole great mouthfuls of mackerel. What was worse was the shark's habit of tearing away pieces of the net along with the fish; if he continued, the men knew, they would be put to great expense to replace the net, and of course they would lose the present catch.

They used normal tactics to frighten sharks away—banging on the boat, splashing and beating the water, and generally making a commotion. But this big shark was not scared; he may have been a veteran of many such attempts to frighten him.

The two men tried to haul the net aboard as quickly as they could, hoping to be too speedy for the shark. But the shark still went on grabbing fish and net and even had a kind of tug-of-war match with them: he held on to the net and shook it with a typical sideways motion. This nearly resulted in one or both of the men falling overboard.

Growing bolder and bolder, the shark came right up to the boat in his attacks. One of the men finally took an oar and struck him very hard on the snout with the butt end. This is usually very discouraging to any shark, as it was to this one; he swam away to a distance.

The men were able to get their net in with its load of mackerel, but suddenly they were frozen stiff with horror: the shark was coming straight at the boat like a torpedo. He either thought this was another way to get a meal or was taking deliberate vengeance. We do not know whether animal reason can understand the latter idea.

At any rate, the shark's blunt head struck amidships with such an impact that a hole about three feet square was torn in the boat's side. Then the shark backed away and cruised round and round the sinking boat, no doubt waiting for another and much larger meal.

The two men signalled frantically for help; in the nick of time another fishing boat came up, took them aboard, and towed the rammed boat to port. The load of mackerel was lost, of course, so the shark did accomplish its evil purpose. When the boat was taken for repairs, a number of teeth were found embedded in the jagged tear in its side. I am glad to say this evidence of shark's ferocity did not discourage the men from going to sea again. A harpooner I know of in Nova Scotia became a farmer after a similarly spine-chilling encounter.

16

A Dream Come True

By the beginning of 1954 the aquarium I was planning with Coppock was beginning to take shape. A company called the Marine Exhibition Corporation had been formed and had negotiated the lease of a piece of land on Virginia Key. This key is connected by the Rickenbacker Causeway to the mainland of Miami and is neighbour to Key Biscayne, the location of a former coconut plantation developed by the Dade County Commission into a public bathing beach and recreation area.

The Corporation negotiated a lease of the land from Dade County, agreed to build and maintain an aquarium there at no cost to the county, and specified that at the end of forty-five years the land, the aquarium, and all improvements would revert to the county, also without cost. Thus even though the aquarium is now private property, in less than forty years it will be run by the representatives of the public and will belong to the people of Miami.

The existence of the aquarium has already been of great help to Dade County because of the number of people it attracts to cross Rickenbacker Causeway. This was built on a loan a few years ago, and although there was a fairly heavy toll, for some time there was not even enough revenue to pay the interest on the loan. However, following the opening of the aquarium, so many cars have crossed the causeway and paid their toll that the time is almost in sight when the loan will have been repaid.

I have purposely been referring to the Seaquarium as the "aquarium" because at this time our dream had no name. In fact we could not think of or agree on a name for such a long time that we finally resorted to a public competition. We got a vast number of entries and such odd suggestions as "Aquarama", "Fish Bowl", "Sea-O-Rama", and, of all things, "Deep Sea Peep See". Of the 21,000 entries from over thirty states, Canada, Mexico, Cuba, and Hawaii, 173 had the same name, the one we liked best. We gave the prize to the first entry bearing this name and christened our project the Miami Seaquarium.

By June, 1954, plans were so advanced that I was officially appointed Director of Collections and Exhibitions. I could not start getting fish because the tanks were not ready to hold water, but there were many things we needed first—rocks, corals, and weeds for background in the tanks.

As soon as there was water in a tank, we would go out and stock it, according to whether it was a tank intended for large specimens or for the smaller reef fish. For about three months at the end of this preparatory period we were working night and day in the keys, on the reefs, over at Bimini, and in the bay near the Seaquarium, bringing in the 18,000 fish which inhabit the various pools and tanks.

At last on September 24, 1955, the Seaquarium was opened. One of the porpoises we had brought in not long before gave birth to a baby in the main tank just before the public began to pass the turnstiles.

But the opening of the Seaquarium did not mean that I just sat back and put my feet up; fish in an aquarium always have to be replaced because they are always dying from one cause or another. Some, as I have said, do not even begin eating in captivity. Expeditions for larger fish are made about every six weeks, while hardly a week goes by without my assistants or myself taking a short trip to a reef or out into the bay to catch leopard rays and trawl with the big net for sea horses.

Of course we are always hoping to come up with a rare fish, as we did with the pigmy angelfish, but we do not always find one in conventional ways. I have my eyes open all the time for fish whenever I am within sight of water. In the trunk of my car is a net, a bucket with a rope on it, and several plastic bags, so that if I see or hear of a fish I am always prepared to take it alive.

12

One of my rarest specimens was collected while crossing the bridge on Rickenbacker Causeway in my car. Along this bridge there are always rows of fishermen, wearing everything from aprons to swimming shorts, and since there is a speed limit of twenty miles per hour, a driver has plenty of time to look at what they have caught. One morning on my way to work at the Seaquarium I saw a man fling over his shoulder on the end of a line a fish which I knew to be rare. It looked to me like a threadfish, about which there is some dispute among ichthyologists, and I wanted it for the Seaquarium. Quickly turning my car round and, I'm afraid, ignoring the speed limit in my haste to get the fish before the man should kill it, I rushed up to him and asked for it. He did not want it; I almost snatched it out of his hand and tried to get some sea water to put it in. The rope on my bucket was not long enough to let it down to the sea from where I was, so hoping that the fish would live, I drove the car to the end of the bridge and got clean sea water there. Then I put the fish in it in a plastic bag, made sure there was enough air in the bag, and drove off—again without regard to the speed limit—to the Seaquarium to put the fish in a holding tank.

To my great relief the fish revived and even began to eat within a few days. A beautiful thing, appearing two-dimensional from the front like a look-down, it was about ten inches long, iridescent silvery-white with green showing through and faint black stripes down its sides. From the dorsal and ventral fins grew long threads, longer than the fish itself, which give it its name. After it had recovered from the shock of capture, we put it in the tank with its cousins the look-downs and the moon-fish; it almost outdid them in beauty.

In the capture and keeping of this fish we were doing a service to ichthyology, for no one knows exactly what this fish is. It is presumed to be the young form of another fish, but there is a dispute as to whether the adult form is the Cuban jack or the African pompano. Ours was the largest threadfish so far captured; thus there is a chance that if we manage to keep it as it grows and observe its changes, we shall find out what the adult is. On the other hand, this fish may be a form which does not reach adulthood in the Atlantic at all, as some ichthyologists have suggested. We shall have to wait and see. At any rate the story of the capture of the threadfish illustrates the unpredictable nature of collecting. You can be on the look-out for a particular specimen for years until by a one-in-a-million chance you find it. This is the source of much of the excitement, surprise—and frustration—of my job.

When you enter the Seaquarium to see the results of this job you walk down a long covered path lined with palms, tropical trees, and flowers, and enter the main building. Here under one roof—or rather, surrounded by one wall, for the tanks are open to the sky—are the main tank, the reef tank, and twenty-six corridor tanks.

The main tank is eighty feet in diameter, seventeen feet deep, and contains 602,000 gallons of sea water pumped from Biscayne Bay. The water, which is filtered in our own plant, passes through this tank at the rate of 3,000 gallons a minute. The amount of water needed daily to fill the needs of the Sea-quarium is well over one million gallons. The nearness of the bay with its vast amounts of water makes the Seaquarium site almost ideal for the maintenance of live fish.

Visitors walk round the corridor surrounding the main tank and look into the water through two tiers of windows. Each of these windows is double because of the great pressure of water on them; between the panes of glass can be seen at either side small tubes of what look like tiny pieces of chalk. These are crystals of a silicone compound which absorbs any condensation between the panes to keep the glass clear.

If you go into the Seaquarium early in the day, you may see a diver inside the tank cleaning these windows with a piece of steel wool like the soap pads a housewife uses to clean her pots and pans. He is removing algae, the omnipresent tiny plants which grow in water all the time. Algae constitute the biggest single problem in keeping the water clear in aquaria; if left untouched, the plants will produce a green slime every-where within two days. Each aquarium has a secret anti-algae formula with which it treats the water in its filtration plant, and we are no exception. All these formulae are based on

copper sulphate, the best anti-algae agent which has been discovered. However, nothing will completely kill algae, although
a good formula will inhibit their growth. Therefore a diver
who cleans windows really is necessary.

The most obvious inhabitants of our main tank are the
porpoises, usually about nine of them. They include Beebe,
who was born in the tank (she is not the baby born on opening day; that one subsequently died). The porpoises swoop
round the diver as he cleans the windows, asking him to play
with them, and they will come to look at you through the glass.
Four times a day they are fed in a spectacular jumping display
which takes place at the top of the tank, where a platform
resembling a Bahama fishing boat has been built. Their trainer
stands at the end of this and holds fish up as the porpoises
jump for them. One porpoise is trained to take a cigarette out
of the trainer's mouth, and another leaps twenty feet in the air
to take a fish the trainer holds above his head while he is standing on an elevation above the platform. Immediately following
this performance, in which the trainer calls to each porpoise by
name, one of two divers goes down into the tank and feeds the
rest of the fish by hand from a basket. The porpoises, not satisfied with their own meal, try in every way to get their snouts
into the basket for second helpings.

The floor of the tank is covered with sand and stones, to
resemble the bottom of the sea; every few weeks a diver uses
an underwater vacuum cleaner to suck up all this sand and the
dirt that has fallen on it so that a fresh supply can be put down.
To make the fish feel as much at home as possible, there are
also on the bottom several large rocks, shells, and clumps of
coral—and the heads of three large brooms, turned upside
down. These broom-heads are for the porpoises to scratch
their backs on; you can see them rolling over and running
their backs along the bristles, then turning round and doing it
again.

In the rocks are a number of large moray eels, which love to
hide in holes from which they just stick out their pointed
heads; because their gills are behind their heads, as they breathe
they appear to be gulping. Between the rocks lurk the three

remaining jewfish, original inhabitants of the Seaquarium. They spend most of their days almost still beside the rocks, occasionally making a slow promenade round the borders of the tank so that people can see their grey, soft scales.

There is usually at least one shark in the tank—sometimes three or four, depending upon how recently the collecting crew has brought some in. These tiger or nurse sharks are not dangerous, although, as I have pointed out, they are not wholly trustworthy. Once we did have to remove some sharks from this tank because the divers were afraid of them, but no diver has been injured.

On the underside of a shark you will often see a small fish striped horizontally black and white, swimming so close to the shark that it looks as if it were stuck to its skin. It is. This shark remora, a strange fish which has on the top of its head an oval sucker looking like part of a Venetian blind, swims under a shark and attaches itself to it by means of the sucker, so that it can pick up the scraps from the shark's meals. In sea life there are a number of examples of creatures pairing so that each can benefit: a hermit crab, for instance, carries sea anemones on top of its borrowed shell, so that the anemone gets the protection of being moved around and the crab gets some of the food the anemone attracts with its waving tentacles. It is not quite clear what benefits the shark gets from its partnership with the remora, but the latter certainly gets at least two—a free ride and a free meal.

Not unlike the remora in appearance is another fish in this tank, the cobia. It is much bigger, reaching about four or five feet in length, but it has the same stripes and a similar arrangement of fins. If you are looking in from the top of the tank, you might also mistake the cobia for a shark, for from this angle it has a similar shape. A cobia is sometimes known as a "crab-eater" because it loves a meal of crabs from the bottom of the sea.

Although sharks are not a great danger to the diver, turtles, of all pacific creatures, often are. This is not because they attack him, but because they are so big and clumsy that they can easily knock him over. They come careening into him as they investigate what he has in his basket of food. If they get hold of anything between their teeth, they are extremely slow to let go: last year one diver's hand got caught by a turtle which simply was not aware of how strong its jaws were; it was some time before the diver could pry them open. Turtles have surprisingly little brain capacity, and they certainly don't appear to use what they have; they bumble round the tank in a slow and aimless fashion, even getting in the way of the porpoises doing their high jumps.

There are usually at least two sawfish gliding slowly round the bottom of the tank and sometimes a dozen leopard rays. We do occasionally have giant manta rays, but I have experienced no success in keeping them for any length of time. There are always several kinds of grunts and snappers, some cousins of the spotted jewfish in the grouper family, and some porgies. Swimming majestically near the surface, as if they knew what aristocrats of the sea they are, are such tarpon and bonefish as I have been able to bring in alive. As I look at them, I remember my former battles with them on the rod and line, but I feel even more proud of these that are living than any I caught and killed.

One question immediately springs to mind about collections of fish living together in conditions as nearly as possible resembling their natural habitats: why don't they eat each other? This they certainly would do in the ocean, and here the opportunities seem to be so much greater. The answer is that they do eat each other, but since they are regularly and well fed by us there is not the same incentive as in the ocean. They also have a curious respect for each other when they have both been in the tank a certain time; it is as if there were a club to which survival brings admittance. When new fish are put into the tank, by some means or other they are immediately recognizable to the other fish. The larger predators, including the porpoises, will chase the newcomers; if they catch one, that's the end of a specimen, but if they don't, there is a good chance the new arrival will survive to become a member of the club. About half of a new set of porgies, for example, will survive. This is why collecting is a full-time job.

Although the large fish in the main tank are dramatic and attract a lot of attention, I personally prefer the smaller ones in the reef tank, which is another circular tank with two tiers of windows. Set to one side and behind the main tank, and connected to it by a clear passage of water called the flume, this tank is also seventeen feet deep, but it is only fifty feet across and holds only 235,000 gallons of water. Its rocks and corals have been built up very high to resemble a natural reef. Because we have reproduced as well as we could the conditions of such a reef, where the large number of varied fish is typical, our tank contains a veritable swarm.

In this tank are several kinds of triggerfish, which have the fascinating spine mechanism. The black triggerfish, I think, is one of the most subtly beautiful of all. It seems to be all one colour until viewed in the light, when a host of deep rich colours, from brown and crimson to green, blue, and even yellow, can be seen. On its back is a long black fin. In shallow water you can see this fin flapping back and forth at the surface with a slapping noise.

We also have many members of the angelfish family, including the queen angelfish, who is blue with a gold edge and wears a crown on top of her head. There are many kinds of trunkfish, all encased in their bony triangular "boxes". In the centre is usually a school of look-downs which slowly revolve and stare disdainfully at the spectator. Near the surface are some more tarpon and dolphins, beautiful streamlined swimmers with long central dorsal fins and large heads. There are also barracudas, who despite their viciousness respect the law of the tanks and confine themselves to preying on newcomers. We have parrotfish of many sizes and colours, pufferfish, porcupine fish, porkfish, and many others. When the diver comes to feed this tank after he has finished in the main tank, the fish settle like a swarm of colourful insects round his basket, following him wherever he goes. Besides fish for the carnivorous residents he brings a cabbage head for the parrotfish and other vegetarians, who find it a very good substitute for marine plants.

Around the corridor surrounding the main exhibits are the

twenty-six tanks I regard as my special pride. In these small tanks, which have a capacity of three to five hundred gallons of water, are to be found the very small fish, many of which, such as the pigmy angelfish and the threadfish, are very rare. The small size of the tanks permits the spectator to get close to and really see every part of the fish. There is a special light for the use of photographers, which can be switched on to show the fish's lovely colours to best advantage.

In the first special tank is a collection of small rays, sting rays, and butterfly rays with their young. There are often births here; you can see the tiny replicas of the parents rippling their circular bodies to move around as soon as they are born. Living with them are sea catfish, whose barbels (filaments) around the mouth locate their food.

The second tank has numbers of moray eels, some spotted and some of one colour, all seeming to gasp as they poke their heads out of the rocks. The next few tanks house reef fish of the same kinds as are to be found in the reef tank. In the seventh tank is the horseshoe crab, a rather frightening creature which evolved early in the history of the animal kingdom and has never developed since; this we know from fossils which exactly resemble the living creature. The horseshoe crab's shell is often a foot across, and many much bigger ones have been seen in the ocean. The crab is shaped not so much like a horseshoe as like a huge hard-shelled bug, with a long tail sticking out behind.

In the ninth tank is a crustacean of surprising appearance, the flame scallop. Inside its half-open shell you can see a gorgeous red colour which gives the scallop its name. The tenth tank is an octopus cave; a number of these extraordinary creatures undulate along the rocks and even walk across the front glass so that you can clearly see their suckers.

In the eleventh tank are what you might at first glance call pyjamafish, for they look as if they are wearing black and white striped pyjamas. They are actually cubbyus, tiny members of the drumfish family, most of whose members make a distinctive noise which gives them their name. Also in this tank are jack-knife fish, who have black and white stripes too, but very much bolder and more brilliant, and a dorsal fin which juts backwards to form a jack-knife shape with the body.

The next three tanks are filled with fresh water, in which we keep fish like the tinsel-covered piranha, which are sufficiently characteristic of Florida to be interesting. Here also are some more catfish, for they are chiefly fresh-water dwellers and never get far from a river mouth. There are also some sunfish, a reminder of my youth, and some Florida garfish, interesting survivals of a breed once more numerous and therefore important to students of evolution. They have elongated mouths full of teeth like a crocodile or alligator, and they can reach a length of twelve feet, with scales so tough that they cannot be pierced with an axe.

In one of these tanks we usually keep electric eels, which are not very attractive and really not very interesting except for their ability to give a nasty shock. They look like long sausages and they move very little. One of these tanks last year was converted to salt water and made into a home for over fifty baby turtles which had been found on one of the beaches near Miami and presented to us. They would flap their tiny flippers and scurry round near the surface of the water, pushing each other out of the way when they were fed. Eventually as they got larger we distributed them among the other tanks.

In the sixteenth tank are jewelfish, tiny fish hardly more than half an inch long, of deepest blue. When the light shines through them you see on their bodies a number of jewel-like spots of a much more intense blue. It is just as if someone had stuck blue sapphires on to them.

Sea horses inhabit the next tank, along with two very curious crustaceans: the arrow crab looks like a great sea-going spider, all legs and very little body, while the coral shrimp looks not unlike it, but has bright bands of red and white on its body and long white legs.

Small reef fish and bottom fish, including deadly-looking scorpionfish, triggerfish, and bottom-crawling flounders, live in the next few tanks. Another tank is devoted to spiny lobsters and huge stone crabs, which have waving tentacles and claws;

still another has tiny creatures like the pigmy angelfish, which outdoes much larger fish in activity.

The last tank is spectacular, for in it are a number of brilliant mauve, puce, and chalky-white sea anemones. They are attached to the rocks with which the tank is lined and wave their tentacles in the current with a graceful motion. Round the rocks flutter a number of very colourful tiny fish: the blue-head wrasse, which in the young form is yellow with a smoky stripe down its side, and in the adult form is blue at the head and green at the tail, with two black bands and a pale blue one separating the two colours; the beau gregory, with its many colours; the yellow-tailed demoiselle, the adult form of the jewelfish. As the jewelfish matures, the spots or jewels move farther apart, and the tail becomes bright yellow. It is not an infrequent phenomenon with reef fish that young and adult should be so different.

As you leave the main building of the Seaquarium, you pass the filtration plant, where you can see the water gushing up in one of our pumping operations. Fish which live in the sea are very fussy about the nature of their water: if you were to put salt into rain water, for example, fish would not live in it, because the sea contains all kinds of salts and compounds besides sodium chloride. And it differs in salinity in different parts. Near the shore the salinity is low because of dilution from rivers, whereas in and around the Gulf Stream the solution is much stronger because the sun's heat evaporates water. This is one reason why, I think, some of our specimens die when they are brought in, for the delicate mechanism of a fish does not find it easy to transfer from one degree of salinity to another. It would, however, be very difficult to arrange different conditions for each species and practically impossible to bring water in from the Gulf Stream.

The pumps at the Seaquarium are worked electrically, but since the lives of nearly 18,000 fish depend on their continual working, we have a diesel pump standing by in case of a power failure. To my relief there has not yet been any need to use it.

Beyond the filtration plant you come to the shark channel, which is 750 feet in circumference with an island in the middle.

You can walk across the channel on bridges to see the sharks swimming beneath. This channel, because of its currents and its spaciousness, simulates ocean conditions. We often have as many as eighty or one hundred sharks in it. They are fed three times a day by an attendant who stands on one of the bridges and lowers fish down to the channel on the end of a rope. The sharks come up and slash at the food with their teeth, pushing each other out of the way in their eagerness.

To the left of the shark channel are the Lost Islands, two pools also with islands in the middle of them. Because these have a water supply directly from the bay, the level of the water rises and falls with the tides. The setting represents tropical islets. On them we have placed iguanas from South America, flamingoes, a species of vulture, and some armadillos. In the water around the islands are sharks, particularly baby ones about two feet long, barracudas, parrotfish, triggerfish, needlefish, bonefish, lobsters, and crabs. Here is perhaps the most natural setting possible for fish in captivity, but of course it does not provide the opportunities for such close observation as the tanks do.

Particularly noticeable on the edge of these tide-pools are the fiddler crabs, busy little creatures an inch or two across, which scurry around the edge without stopping. The males carry a huge left claw which they wave as they run sideways; the females do not have this claw. It is in the tide-pools that the peculiar rowing action of the parrotfish may be seen best by watching from the top, as they graze among the underwater vegetation.

Just beside the Lost Islands is the manatee pool, where two manatees can be seen slowly cruising round and round, or just lying on the bottom. Occasionally they rise to the surface and puff as they breathe. Their cabbage—for they are vegetarians—is kept in a wire cage which they have to push down to get their food; this arrangement keeps the pool clean and the sea cows a little more active than they would normally be.

Coming back to the main building, you find the Seashow Arena, where trained porpoises and sea lions give three performances every day. They are taught by Adolf Frohn, who was a friend of mine at Marine Studios, and who is the first man in the world to train a performing porpoise. He has schooled them to jump through hoops, ring bells, play ball, and even shoot baskets. The trainer is at a great disadvantage with porpoises in that they are in the water and he on dry land, but Frohn has overcome this handicap by persuading the porpoises to do what they should with gifts of fish.

Spectators at the performances sit on a tier of seats in a kind of amphitheatre looking down on a very deep pool at their feet. Over their heads is a geodesic dome erected last year after the one covering the American exhibition at the Moscow Fair had been such a success.

Behind the arena are tanks containing more sea lions and some delightful harbour seals which came from California and are one of our few exhibits not native to Florida. These seals sit like little old men straight up in the water and look at you with their curious opaque eyes, waiting to see if you have any fish for them.

On the way back into the main building you will see a large model of the sunfish we once put into the big tank, only to have it die shortly afterwards. The model was made in the same way as the scientists modelled the giant manta ray during Leon Mandel's Galapagos expedition: they took casts of it and built the creature up from them.

At the back of the shark channel is the dock where we keep our collecting equipment and where we are delighted to have the public watch us unload our catch. There is a huge hoist here for moving heavy fish from the live-wells to the waiting trucks, and there are great racks where we dry and mend nets when porpoises and rays have done their worst to tangle and break them.

Incidentally, we launched, last year, a collecting boat which is regarded as the most advanced vessel of its kind. The *Seaquarium I* has a special door in the stern for sea-dwelling passengers to swim right into. The live-well inside, twenty-one feet long, eight feet wide, and three feet deep, can accommodate and retain in good condition anything from a jewelfish to a whale. These specimens never have to be taken out of the water from the time they are caught to the time they reach the Seaquarium docks.

Also behind the shark channel is a huge refrigerator and freezer, where we keep supplies of food for our specimens. We buy 67 tons of fish a year to feed them at the rate of 5 or 6 hundredweight a day. These fish are of the same quality as is sold in food markets, so the supply is naturally very expensive, but it is essential if we are to avoid the risk of poisoning our captives. We buy the fish in huge quantities in the parts of the country where they are abundant at a particular time, and therefore less expensive: squid in Massachusetts, herring and whiting in Maine, butterfish in New Jersey, and blue runner in Florida. At Miami we have another huge freezer from which we replenish ours at the Seaquarium. We are careful to vary the diet of the fish as much as possible.

Behind the main corridor behind the twenty-six corridor tanks are some very important parts of the Seaquarium. Three plain concrete holding tanks with a stream of water constantly flowing through them are used for new small fish to acclimatize themselves to captivity. They often make attempts to escape: the threadfish, for instance, as soon as it was put in the holding tank, took a precipitous rush to the surface in an attempt to jump out.

We also put any fish in these tanks which we think is not well, for fish at close quarters with one another will begin to pick on any one of their number which may look sick. Then, if we can, we treat the fish in our laboratory, which is also situated behind the corridor tanks. The best way of treating a sick fish is to allow it to swim in a very weak chemical solution, but you have to be very careful that the solution is not so strong as to kill the fish as well as the disease. It is possible to give larger creatures, like porpoises and sharks, medicine in their fish: one porpoise last year was receiving doses of penicillin hidden in blue runner in order to cure a skin disease on its tail.

In the laboratory there is also a complicated apparatus for photographing fish. You might think that there would be little difficulty in doing this when you have fish near you in tanks, but to get a photograph which will show each detail for the purpose of ichthyological study is not so easy. We have rigged up a special tank, whose walls are very close to each other so that the fish cannot turn round while it is being photographed, although it has ample room for movement up and down and sideways. A supply of water is constantly flowing through this tank. Even with this apparatus, the camerman often complains that just as he has focused the fish in the centre of the picture, it moves off again; much patience is needed before a good photograph is produced.

Since for the larger fish the holding tanks are not big enough, we put them in the flume, which is a clear stretch of water between the reef and the main tanks. The only difficulty is that the flume is more than twenty feet above the ground, so that we have to hoist our larger specimens up to it in wooden boxes. We keep sharks, porpoises, rays, and turtles in the flume until they begin eating; then we put them into the main tank by opening a gate leading into it, or into other pools by hoisting them down again.

Since I am director of exhibitions as well as collections, it is my duty to see that fish are placed in tanks where they will be as healthy as possible. This does not always mean placing them in an entirely natural setting: a shark, for instance, would be perfectly at home in the reef tank, but in a few moments not many reef fish would be left. We tend to keep larger fish separate from smaller ones, and in the corridor tanks they have been grouped as far as possible in families, or into divisions of similar kinds. For instance, the demoiselles or damselfish, which are so very pretty in their bright colours, are not charming in their manners; they have to be kept separate from certain other small fish which they will attack.

During the five years of its existence, the Seaquarium has been visited by an average of 750,000 people a year. Parties of schoolchildren frequently come on educational trips; once we had 2,000 of them in a week. There are no peak periods for the Seaquarium—people come steadily throughout the year—with one exception. Our staff has no idea what Christmas is, for at that time the people who are on brief vacations in Florida flock to the Seaquarium in thousands.

Although we have no laboratory equipped for research, we have been able to be of great help to a number of institutions, who send people to use our fish for experiments or to whom we send material. Dr. Perry Gilbert of Cornell University has been using our sharks for a number of years for experiments on the pituitary gland; he comes to the Seaquarium to inject them with his latest solution and to check on the results about three times a year. Woods Hole Marine Laboratory on Cape Cod, Massachusetts, has been trying for a long time to find a suitable tag to use on fish in the study of their migrations; some substance which will neither hurt the fish nor fall off is needed. We have used many of the suggested materials on our specimens.

In research to find a shark repellent suitable for inclusion in lifeboats and life-saving equipment on boats and aeroplanes, a number of universities have been co-operating with the United States Navy and Air Force. We are often asked to try their discoveries on our sharks, or to contribute materials they think might give the secret.

The Marine Laboratory of the University of Miami, our nearest neighbour on Virginia Key, was at one time helping the Navy in research on underwater sounds. A few staff members brought recording apparatus and put a microphone into the main tank to take tapes of the numerous noises porpoises make under water.

For cancer research, we frequently supply sea urchins to various universities; the Cancer Institute of Miami has asked us for fish livers. Urologists often want live sea horses for study of kidney disorders, for the sea horse is one of the few marine creatures with functioning kidneys.

Sharks are used in attempts to find an anaesthetic for fish and in research on enzymes, the digestive catalysts present in the alimentary tract. A member of the chemistry department at Harvard University, who wanted shark bile for his experiments, offered to go with me to catch the sharks and even to bring his own milk can for the bile!

A group of doctors at the University of California in Los Angeles are beginning a study of a children's disease called marble bone, in which the bone develops without a marrow cavity. When they found that the manatee is one of the few creatures whose bones have no marrow cavities, they asked us for dead manatees to dissect. We eventually managed to supply such a manatee, and I am hoping to be able to ship them a live one as soon as I can.

For university museums we often supply preserved specimens. For example, the Museum of Comparative Zoology at Harvard asked us for a frozen cobia, and Presbyterian University—St. Luke's Hospital—wanted a toadfish. We are often asked to advise schools and colleges on the construction of aquaria, which we sometimes stock completely with specimens shipped by air or rail.

The transportation of live fish is an operation which has benefited by the advance of modern technology. In my early collecting days, I had to send fish in tin tanks and run the risk of having them arrive upside down with the fish dead. But now the use of heavy plastic bags and oxygen means there is more than an even chance that the fish will arrive in good condition.

When we are going to send small fish, or even sharks only about two feet long, we put two plastic bags, one inside the other, into large cardboard boxes, clearly marked *live fish*. In the inner one we put the fish and enough water to cover them, tie the top, and insert a tube from a cylinder of oxygen. When the bag is inflated, we remove the tube and tie the bag as tightly as possible. The other bag is also tied tightly; it is a safety measure in case the inner one should break. When the box is sealed, the fish are rushed to a railway station or airport. According to the species they will be safe for periods up to twenty-four hours.

Packing fish to fly long distances, arranging them in tanks, treating them when they are sick—all are part of a day at the Seaquarium. I am so frequently at sea with the collecting fleet that there is always a huge backlog of such jobs waiting for me when I arrive in dock. But since for me the Seaquarium is a dream come true, a place where people can see fish as I have seen and known them all my life, such jobs are never chores. And—who knows?—one day I may even have the task of looking after a whale!

My varied endeavours recently included paving the way for a celebrated porpoise romance. Since the first printing of this book went to press I've had the unprecedented and difficult task of transporting a $4\frac{1}{2}$-hundredweight porpoise via land, sea and air from the Miami Seaquarium to the Adriatic shore. The way this came about was that the mayor of Miami forwarded to the Seaquarium the following heart-rending appeal from Mr. Dante Matassoni, president of the tourist office of Cesenatico, a small Italian seaside resort on the north coast of the Adriatic:

Dear Sir,

Please pardon me if I'm importunating you with my peculiar request, which—by the other hand it is very important to me and my fellow-citizien! It is on behalf of our dophin, who is living here in Cesenatico in the "Vena Mazzarini"—a sort of a Canal with a promenade—where it makes the joy of our children and, I can say, even of grown-up people! Now, our dophin, who happened to be a femal-dophin, feels very lonely and, thogh she's still looking well, she's visibly suffering of nostalgia by lac of companionship!

We can't get here, nowhere a dophin-man, nor can we afford to buy one! . . . yet we are afraid our "Lalla" (that is the name of our dophin!) may die! . . . that's why we do apply to you, sir! Somebody told us, you have some dophins up there . . . would you, and could you, be so kind to send us a dophin-man?! . . .

This appeal was so touching it could not be ignored. Also, realizing the publicity value of such an undertaking, we thought it well worth trying for this reason alone. Could it be done? We thought so and agreed to try it. How? That became my problem, and I set out to make arrangements to bring one of our males to Italy. Naturally, the event came into the headlines, and the *Miami News* sponsored a contest to find an appropriate name for our porpoise. The contest was limited to children twelve years of age and under. Among the thousands of names submitted, the name "Palooza" cropped up a hundred times (the contest winner was selected by a drawing held later), so that was the name by which the world's most glamorized porpoise became known.

With transportation arrangements scheduled on the Italian luxury liner *Augustus*, Cliff Ball, Seaquarium manager, and myself rode on a truck with Palooza resting on a sponge-rubber mattress to the Miami Airport. We transferred him to a National cargo plane and were flying north by 7 p.m. On the plane we nursed him as though he were an invalid. He stood the handling well during the eight-hour flight to Idle-wild Airport, New York, where we arrived in the teeming rain and terrific winds of a hurricane called "Bertha". As arranged beforehand, Dr. Christopher Coates, Director, and Aage Olsen, Superintendent, from the New York Aquarium were waiting to transport the Palooza party via truck to shipside. Here, at 3.30 a.m., we were able to press some newsmen and photographers into helping us make the transfer from the plane on to the waiting truck. We rode through the downpour to the West 44th Street Pier, where the *Augustus* was loading cargo. Two hundredweight of frozen fish for Palooza was taken aboard.

Amid great confusion we were able to have our large rubber tank hoisted on to the foredeck and partially filled with water. Afraid to chance the crane, we carried our charge on a stretcher up the stairs and placed him in the tank. At this point we were all as wet as the porpoise, but not as happy about it. We were relieved to see that Palooza seemed to be in good condition. Of course, he had been kept thoroughly wet during the whole trip. A press party round Palooza's pool had been scheduled for 10 a.m., but because of the storm we did not expect any attendance. However, we underestimated New York newsmen and their intrepid coverage of a significant story. About twenty-five gathered round, with cameras shielded by their raincoats, as an attractive Spanish dancing girl placed a bridal wreath on Palooza's head.

So far, so good. But my troubles were not over. My wife, Sally, who was to accompany Cliff and me on the voyage, had left Miami on a passenger flight scheduled to arrive at New York in time to taxi to the steamship dock before 8 a.m. By eleven, there was still no sign of Sally. Her plane had not been able to land at LaGuardia Field and went back to Newark, New Jersey. She finally made it, though, by bus and taxi, just before sailing time.

The *Augustus* cast off at noon with bands blasting away and streamers, ribbons and flowers appearing in spite of the rain. This was a *bon voyage* for the 800 passengers among whom Palooza was numbered.

The ship glided down North River and was well out to sea when darkness came on. We were somewhat relieved to be on the second leg of our journey. The ocean was very rough, and the ship rolled considerably all night. Many passengers were seasick, including Palooza. I was seriously worried and stayed with him all night, holding his head up to make his breathing easier, and patting him to give him encouragement. I am sure this helped, because his actions indicated that he appreciated my attention and company. The next day he seemed brighter, and by mid-day the sea had moderated considerably. Palooza took a couple of mackerel from my hand and seemed to feel much better. So did I. As Cliff came to relieve me for a two-hour watch, I thought, "Now I can enjoy some food and rest myself."

All was going well as the *Augustus* anchored off Gibraltar to ferry ashore passengers and cargo. However, she was five hours behind schedule, and Genoa, our port of debarkation, was a good three days' run across the Mediterranean, allowing for a stop at Naples. We were due there at 5 p.m. next day. Now it would be about 9 p.m. This caused us great concern, as well as disappointment. The Italian officials had arranged to have a U.S. Navy Band welcome our arrival with Palooza. Because of our late arrival this was cancelled, but our arrival in the harbour was very thrilling anyway. We docked close to the U.S.S. *Saratoga,* which was lighted up like a little city. Late as we were, there were a great many newsmen and cameramen there to meet us. They made notes for their stories and took many photos of us and Palooza. One would think that our Palooza was a conquering hero returning from the wars. The interest and excitement this animal caused was beyond all comprehension. It all seemed as though we were in another world, not just on another continent.

The *Augustus* cleared the harbour about midnight and set a course for Genoa. If all went well we should arrive about 9 p.m. Our fears for Palooza's welfare were greatly relieved by now—but not completely, to be sure. The most frightening and critical part of the journey lay ahead.

From Genoa we would have to endure a 400-mile ride across Italy by motor truck over mountainous winding roads. This meant practically a non-stop run if we were to arrive for the wedding, which was scheduled for 5 p.m. next day. We knew that if we did not make it in time our mission would be a miserable failure. Personally, I would not care to re-experience our tenseness at this point.

Amid gleaming lights our ship crept slowly into the port of Genoa. A blazing reception awaited us. Heading the reception committee were the Mayor of Cesenatico and Dante Matassoni, also a horde of newsmen and photographers representing not only Italian papers but also American, English and French. Art Buchwald, who writes a widely syndicated news column, had come down from Paris to accompany us on the last leg of our journey.

When the ship was tied to the pier, all was ready to hoist Palooza's tank, which had been partially drained to reduce its weight. We had Palooza's Customs, immigration and vaccination documents ready, so there was no delay in unloading. We all held our breath as the ship's derrick groaned. The tank, with Palooza inside, was swung clear of the ship and the waiting truck backed into place. The tank was then lowered until it rested on the truck.

The delegation from Cesenatico beamed with pleasure and satisfaction as they greeted us. Lively march music filled the air. Cameras clicked, flares blazed for the television cameras, and flash bulbs popped. Hordes of citizens attempting to climb on to the truck for a glimpse of Palooza made progress somewhat difficult. Water was pumped into the tank until it was deep enough for Palooza's comfort; there was no lost motion and no time to waste. A half-dozen motor-cycle police blasted their sirens to clear the way as our motorcade lined up behind to proceed through the city. A prince or king could not have had more acclaim than our Palooza, or have been awarded a more spectacular reception.

It was nearly midnight when our caravan reached the outskirts of Genoa. Motor-cycle police led the procession and cleared the highway, halting traffic to let us pass.

I rode in the truck beside the driver. Next came the long black limousine occupied by Mr. Matassoni, who had masterminded the whole programme, Sally, Cliff, and Art Buchwald, who by now had been appointed "best man" for the wedding. A dozen other cars loaded with officials filled out the line. Motor police in autos brought up the rear.

To drive a large truck carrying a load of water weighing several tons with a valuable live creature in it is quite different from hauling a load of solid freight, especially over rough and steep mountain roads at night. I swallowed my heart many times during the first few hours of travel. To me, minutes seemed like hours as we rode along in the darkness. I knew no Italian words so I could say nothing to relieve the tension. The driver operated the truck from the right-hand side of the cab, which added to my uneasiness. The motorcade came to a halt occasionally so I could see how Palooza was taking the ride. I could not see him beneath the water in the darkness, but I would listen nervously until his head came up for a breath of air; I spent some suspense-filled moments waiting to hear that familiar puff.

Our route led 200 miles north to Milan, where we skirted the city and came on to a good highway leading to Cesenatico. This was my first sight of Italy in daylight, and the countryside was beautiful. We noticed posters along the way displaying a large picture of Palooza and announcing the wedding-to-be.

An official car now led the procession, flying the American and Italian flags. A cheering populace lined the highways waving banners and balloons as we passed through the many small towns. This was far more than we had expected. Nearing the end of our journey, with the bridegroom alive, well, and happy, our relief from the severe tension was out of bounds.

Amid cheering and flag-waving we rode into Cesenatico, feeling like heroes indeed. However, the greatest surprise of all awaited us when we reached Lalla's canal. A crowd of at least 10,000 spectators lined the banks of the canal to greet us. It seems the event had been broadcast as an important international affair, and people came from miles away to witness the wedding.

A stage had been erected and draped with flags and flowers from which the officials would conduct the ceremonies. Our truck with the groom in his tank backed between the stage and the canal. Then, amid the cheering of the excited crowd, Palooza went down the aisle (slid down a gangplank) into the canal. At this point excitement really ran high. Along with the bridal wreath, roses and other flowers were tossed into the canal by the hundreds.

Our party were honoured guests upon the stage, and the thoughtful Mayor presented Sally with a beautiful bouquet of flowers. Also on stage was the town's acclaimed most beautiful girl, Chichi Lorenzi—Miss Cesenatico. She sliced and served the huge wedding cake. While we were being praised and flattered by the officials for our accomplishment of bringing "Palooza, King of the Caribbean" 7,500 miles from Miami, Florida, to wed "Lalla, Queen of the Adriatic", the spectators cheered wildly. They jammed and shoved to get a better view, and at least six people were accidently pushed into the canal. This just added to the merriment.

Lalla's joy was unbounded. It was clearly a case of love at first sight. When she spied her mate she sped to his side and displayed her interest by bumping, biting, and tail-slapping. They raced about like a pair of playful puppies. These antics delighted the crowd. Just to show off, Palooza leaped six feet into the air several times, to the cheers of the wedding guests.

The excitement, interest and applause went on and on until darkness closed out the scene. The name Palooza had become a byword, and was heard wherever one happened to be.

The good people of Cesenatico did everything possible to make us enjoy our visit, and they succeeded magnificently.

This whole episode was by far the most challenging and the most rewarding of my career in collecting and handling the creatures of the sea.